CYPRESS INSTITUTE OF RELIGION
9470 Holder
Cypress, California 90630
828-2971

In
Search
of Lehi's
Trail

Published by Deseret Book Company   Salt Lake City, Utah   1976

In Search of Lehi's Trail

Lynn M. Hilton
Hope Hilton

Photography by Gerald W. Silver

Contents

Foreword

For readers of the Bible, who are now thousands of years and many miles removed from its culture and locales, that book of sacred scripture comes more easily to life when we can see photographs of the mountains, valleys, and towns of Palestine as well as the areas of the Roman world into which the gospel of the New Testament was carried.

Modern Church history means more to us when we see the New York, Ohio, Missouri, and Illinois environs where the Church was restored through the Prophet Joseph Smith, where important revelations dealing with the restoration were given by heavenly messengers, and where the early members of The Church of Jesus Christ of Latter-day Saints labored to reestablish the kingdom of God on earth.

However, the areas through which Lehi and his family traveled in their journey from the Holy Land to the Western Hemisphere have remained elusive and only in the imagination until now. For nearly a century and a half readers of the Book of Mormon have been able to travel only in their mind's eye with Lehi as he led his family from Jerusalem southward to the Red Sea coast, where they turned inland, then crossed through "much affliction" before coming to a coastal area they described as "bountiful." Readers have had to contemplate only in their imaginations that historic journey, the places where Lehi's party stopped, where they built their ship, where they landed in the Western Hemisphere, in their promised land.

Because of this, the editors of the *Ensign* considered, when the Church announced its eight-year adult gospel curriculum of scripture study, how they could best support this inspired call to "search the scriptures." The idea to investigate the general area of Lehi's journey soon presented itself as a companion study of the Book of Mormon, and in 1972 discussions started on the likelihood of such a venture.

The plan was to photograph the area outlined by Dr. Hugh Nibley in his series "Lehi in the Desert," published in the *Improvement Era* in 1950. After learning more about Dr. Nibley's reasons for identifying the general locales of Lehi's journey, the *Ensign* staff began to plan how to travel through the Arabian peninsula. A look at the map of that area indicated that Lehi's trail went through lands that are politically difficult to enter today, lands culturally misunderstood by many in the Western world.

After considerable inquiry, we determined that not just anyone could make this trek today. It required someone who not only loved and understood the Book of Mormon, but who also knew and understood the Arab world, who could speak

Arabic, who had experience in traveling there, and who could devote several months to the venture.

The names of Lynn M. and Hope Hilton came to mind. Their credentials for the trip were impressive. Brother Hilton, with a Ph.D. from the University of Chicago in educational administration, had spent eleven years in adult education at Brigham Young University, including directing many travel study tours. Subsequently he spent twelve years as co-owner of a travel-study firm, which took him dozens of times to Europe, the Middle East, Africa, and Asia. Since then they have established several business enterprises in Cairo, Egypt.

We approached the Hiltons with the idea of investigating the possible locales of Lehi's journey in Arabia, and they were delighted to accept. Gerald W. Silver, a photographer for the *Deseret News*, was asked to accompany them.

After approval for the project had been given, and as the departure date neared, progress of the preparatory work was reviewed by Dean Larsen, editor of Church magazines. Then Elder Robert D. Hales, Assistant to the Council of the Twelve and managing director of the Church's Internal Communications Department, accepted an invitation to give a blessing to the travelers for their safety and success.

Brother and Sister Hilton and Brother Silver took an idea and turned it into a memorable adventure story. Their conclusions are tentative, of course; the Church does not have an official view on the matter. As Brother and Sister Hilton have said, "Until someone finds a sign saying 'I, Lehi, was here,' our report will always be in the realm of a respectable possibility. But we think that we found far more than we Latter-day Saints ever knew existed concerning Lehi's route. We think our adventure not only illuminates some of the vital elements of the Book of Mormon story, but also throws new light on the contributions of Arab culture to the Book of Mormon."

This fascinating Mormon odyssey was first presented in the September and October 1976 issues of the *Ensign*. We were pleased that Deseret Book Company agreed to publish as a book the Hiltons' account of their research and adventure, and members of the *Ensign* staff assisted in developing this fuller version from the *Ensign* articles. Included here are many additional details and photographs and much useful background for you to enjoy and preserve as a valuable reference.

Jay M. Todd
Managing Editor
The Ensign

Preface

Lynn was working in his office in Salt Lake City when the telephone call that was to alter our lives came to Hope at our home on September 9, 1975. In anticipation of a family move to Cairo, Egypt, the following June, we had just moved three days before from a rather large home to an undersized fifty-year-old bungalow, and Hope was still in the process of fitting our furniture into half as much space when the telephone range. Jay Todd, managing editor of the *Ensign,* was calling, and when he learned Lynn was not at home, he asked Hope to relay the message.

The abbreviated, rather matter-of-fact assignment that was to dramatically change our lives took a full week to make its impact: "Follow in the steps of Lehi from Jerusalem to the land called Bountiful—if you can discover where that might have been." This was the task. Were we willing to undertake it? On September 19 we officially accepted the challenge in Brother Todd's office, after we had determined from business associates and our teenage son, Ralph, that leaving town for five weeks would not totally disrupt their lives. In ten days we had made a tentative plan.

Brother Todd didn't need to tell us such a trip had never been tried in the 146 years since the publication of the Book of Mormon. As avid readers of Church books, we knew no past histories or journals existed: we were starting from scratch with a reference here and there, mostly in obscure books, about the southward journey of the prophet Lehi's family in 600 B.C.

Immediately after the call, Hope began telephoning and corresponding with her Arab friends in Salt Lake City and around the world, telling them of our proposed trip and asking for their advice. Over the years since 1961, when we had made our first joint trip to the Middle East as directors of the initial Brigham Young University Bible Lands tour, she had been accumulating Arab friends. She was intrigued by their culture and history and by the people themselves. After our first trip she began corresponding with three people in the Middle East, and these three had grown to an overwhelming 110 by the fall of 1975, fourteen trips later. Many of these friends were to contribute greatly to the success of our journey. They were the ones who opened our eyes to crucial historical facts, many never yet printed. In addition, they were to help with visa problems and hotel accommodations when regular avenues failed.

Our five-week "Lehi safari" proved to be a peak experience in our lives, an unsurpassed spiritual experience. And our long-time interest in the Middle East, piqued by love of the prophet Nephi and his great accomplishments, made the four months of preparations for this interesting journey pass rapidly. Almost before we were ready, it was time to board the airplane with Jerry Silver and his cameras and fly to a part of the world we had both learned to love. Our hope as we write of our experience is that the knowledge we gained will help others enjoy the Book of Mormon more and will increase their testimonies of the truthfulness of that book.

Lynn and Hope Hilton

Acknowl-edgments

As important as the information we collected from our research were the interpretations of that research and the new insights and information shared willingly by a host of friends. We especially would not have been able to succeed without the second-mile efforts and cooperation of Salim Saad of Amman, Jordan; Angie Chukri of Cairo, Egypt; Hassib Dajani of Jiddah, Saudi Arabia; Sheik Helwan Habtar of Abha, Saudi Arabia; Sa'adi Fatafitah of Tarqumia, Westbank; and Nabeel Mustakim of Jerusalem.

Ladd and Barbara Petty of Salt Lake City supplemented our local library research with research in the Los Angeles Public Library. Interviews with Middle East scholars at both the University of Utah and Brigham Young University prepared our minds for the task ahead. Insight came from Dr. Sami Hanna, Dr. Assiz Atiya, Dr. Sidney Sperry, Dr. Ross T. Christensen, Dr. Hugh Nibley, and Dr. LaMar Berrett. Our thanks also to Eugene England for invaluable assistance in putting our manuscript into book form.

This beforehand research was invaluable, yet we knew that an on-the-spot appraisal (guided by knowledgeable people) and good photographic records would be worth 10,000 words. Accompanying us to record the experience on film was Gerald W. Silver, Salt Lake City photographer, chosen not only for his photographic skills but also his experience as an outdoorsman. Our daughter, Cynthia, of Washington, D. C., an experienced world traveler and keen observer at age 25, added greatly to the adventure's enjoyment and success.

12

The Challenge

J ust consider the scope of the challenge! We were to follow a trail that had been cooling for more than 2,500 years, a trail that lay half a world away in sometimes wartorn territory, now crossing the borders of Israel, Jordan, Saudi Arabia, Yemen, and Oman. All the clues to Lehi's route are contained in a mere eighteen chapters that Nephi wrote years after his journey; and the main purpose of that record was not to record geography and caravan routes, but those marvelous visions given to his father and later to himself.

Then consider our own qualifications. We loved the Middle East, had many friends there, had visited its cities often, and had studied its languages, history, and culture; but we did not have advanced degrees in Middle Eastern studies. We loved the Book of Mormon and had sincere testimonies of its truthfulness, but we were not sophisticated scholars in that field either. But we had an assignment, articulated in blessings pronounced on our heads by Elder Robert D. Hales, who, upon learning of the assignment given to us, wanted to meet us and learn of our preparations and expectations, and who then graciously accepted our request for a blessing. Among other ideas communicated, Elder Hales said: "I bless you with perceptive minds, that as you listen to stories around the campfires and as you hear what your friends tell you and as you see what is before you, you will understand its significance for the Book of Mormon. You will find evidence for Lehi's journey that will strengthen the testimonies of the Saints and convince youth of the truthfulness of the Book of Mormon record and spread the gospel among the Arab people."

We knew that the Book of Mormon was true, and so we started from that premise: what Nephi wrote actually did happen. Inspired by God, Mormon had included Nephi's own record without abridging it. Inspired by God, Joseph Smith had translated it, literally and faithfully. The hypotheses and conclusions we will present are, of course, tentative; it will take archaeologists and historians to provide further supporting evidence. But the story of our search for Lehi's route is an exciting adventure, one that has resulted in some basic conclusions as they relate to actual geographic locales mentioned in the Book of Mormon.

Prior to our journey, we had wondered if our friends in the Middle East would accept our assignment and help us accomplish our goal. They did. They did more. They accepted the goal itself. Mrs. Rihab Ouri of Beirut, a good Muslim friend, summed up the kind of cooperation we received in a letter written after our return: "Did you find the early Mormons of

"... I will go and do ..."

The history of Arabia is written with water, not ink. Where there is water, there is life—that is the inescapable fact of Arabian life—and the great oases of the Arabian peninsula do not move from place to place.

Saudi Arabia?" She had made the connection before we had—that one of the sources of our religion was the Middle East, already the cradle of Christianity, Judaism, and Islam.

One of the encouraging factors in our search was the discovery of the great timelessness of the Arabian peninsula. It is a changeless place, not only geographically but also culturally. It is hard for people in highly developed areas of the world to imagine a place staying the same for two thousand years. We look at the world from our twentieth century perspective in which technology's immense power transforms landscapes into cities within weeks. But technology's impact has not reached much of Arabia.

The history of Arabia is written with water, not ink. Where there is water, there is life—that is the inescapable fact of Arabian life—and the great oases of the Arabian peninsula do not move from place to place. Cities cannot thrive in the desert, and there is a limit to how far suburbs can extend from the central wells and springs. For us, trained in the short time-spans of journalistic history, a surprise came in the way Arabs talk about the three major events of the last 2,500 years of Arabian history. They refer to these events with knowledgeable familiarity, as though they took place yesterday:

1. *The breaking of the Marib Dam.* Not long before Lehi, some heroic but nameless leader undertook the gigantic engineering feat of constructing this dam or dike. Some experts think that the builders were the Sabean kings and that their kingdom was ancient Sheba, where the Queen of Sheba who visited Solomon came from. (1 Kings 10.)[1] They date the building of the dam from 750 B.C.[2] Rainwater diverted by this dam or dike increased the agricultural fertility of up to 4,000 acres of the land until it supported a significant population.[3]

According to the foremost scholar of the subject, the Marib Dam broke in the sixth century A.D.[4] Many survivors of the resultant flood, faced with starvation, fought their way north, carving out with the sword a place for themselves among the central and northern Arabian clans or families and creating social chaos and hostility. The wars that followed lasted centuries. Families in Arabia today still remember that they came from Marib and refer to the breaking of the dam as

---

[1]See Gus W. Van Beek, "The Rise and Fall of Arabia Felix," *Scientific America*, December 1969, p. 41.
[2]Fr. Eugene Hoade, *East of the Jordan* (Jerusalem: Franciscan Printing Press, 1966), p. 318.
[3]Van Beek, p. 43.
[4]Van Beek, p. 39.

though it had happened in their grandfather's time. Its ruins still lie in the southwest corner of Arabia in Yemen.

2. *The life of the prophet Muhammed.* Muhammed's religious mission in the seventh century A.D. resulted in millions of conversions across thousands of miles from India to Spain. For the first time, religion united Arabs and their neighbors across the barriers of waterless sand. Muhammed brought an age of enlightenment that had a direct impact on the Renaissance in Europe.[5]

3. *The discovery of oil.* Thirteen centuries after Muhammed, in the 1940s, the discovery of oil brought the legendary riches of King Midas to countries where donkeys and camels, mud-brick houses, and goat-hair tents had been the measurement of wealth. Now wells can be drilled, pipelines constructed, vast areas and many people freed from the oases' limitations.

But between these three events, Arab memory floats over legendary and contemporary battles, the reign of kings, good harvests and bad droughts. All events, past, present, and future, are *inshalla* (God wills it), and a thousand years is little different from a hundred. The Lord knew the when, how, and where of Lehi's journey. As readers of the Book of Mormon, we started out knowing the why and the when. And we were determined to piece together whatever clues we could find that might aid our understanding of the *how* and the *where.*

The Record of Nephi

We started with the Book of Mormon. Read along with us as we discover what it tells us about that journey, and consider some of the kinds of questions that came to our minds as we pored over these passages from First Nephi.

First, in chapter one, we read that Lehi had "dwelt at Jerusalem in all his days." (V. 4.) Did *at* Jerusalem mean something different from *in* Jerusalem? A few verses later, Lehi "went forth," then "returned to his own house at Jerusalem." (Vv. 6, 7.) Does this mean that he went out of Jerusalem, then came back to Jerusalem? What business would take him forth from Jerusalem?

In chapter 2, the Lord commands Lehi to "depart into the wilderness." (V. 2.) What would wilderness mean to Lehi? Later they leave "the land of his inheritance, and his gold, and his silver, and his precious things." (V. 4.) Why not at least take some money to buy provisions? Or does this mean only that they

---

[5]See Philip K. Hitti, *The Arabs: A Short History* (Chicago: Henry Regnery Co., 1966), p. 187.

left their *objects* of gold and silver? Lehi "took nothing with him, save it were his family, and provisions, and tents." (V. 4.) What kind of provisions might the people carry? How would they travel with tents? Would this life-style be anything like the nomadic life of the Bedouins in contemporary Arabia?

Some clues about direction are in verse 5 of chapter 2: "And he came down by the borders near the shore of the Red Sea; and he traveled in the wilderness in the borders which are nearer the Red Sea." What is the difference between "borders near" and "borders nearer"? At least the Red Sea is a definite landmark. Is there a trail that goes "near" and "nearer"?

In the next verse the account specifies that "when he had traveled three days in the wilderness, he pitched his tent in a valley by the side of a river of water." (V. 6.) That seems to mean three days of traveling in the wilderness *after* they reached the Red Sea, not three days from Jerusalem. Would it be possible to identify that river and that valley?

In verse 8 is an even more specific clue: "[The river] emptied into the Red Sea; and the valley was in the borders near the mouth thereof." Is it possible that Lehi's tents could have been inland from the Red Sea? This is the valley he called Lemuel and the river he called Laman, and in describing it we get a few more clues: ". . . the river emptied into the fountain of the Red Sea." Does *fountain* suggest anything special? And Lehi told Laman that he should be "like unto this river, continually running into the fountain of all righteousness!" (V. 9.) Are there any continually running rivers in Arabia? Lehi wanted Lemuel to be "like unto this valley, firm and steadfast, and immovable in keeping the commandments of the Lord!" (V. 10.) Is there a particular valley that would best fit that description? Then Nephi writes, "And my father *dwelt* in a tent." (V. 15; italics added.) Was this meant to imply some kind of long-term arrangement?

When the journeys back and forth to Jerusalem begin, the record takes some interesting turns of language. For example, when Nephi and his brothers went for the brass plates, they took their tents and went "up to the land of Jerusalem." (3:9.) Why did they take their tents with them? And was Jerusalem "up" from all points of the compass? They ran into problems with Laban and decided to go "down to the land of our inheritance" and collect some of the gold and silver they had left. (V. 22.) Then they "went up again" to Laban's house in Jerusalem. (V. 23. See also 4:4, 34-35; 5:1.) This is intriguing. To where would they go "down" to get to the land of their inheritance after they had gone "up" to Jerusalem? Was "down" in the same direction for both the wilderness and the land of their inheritance? And how far were they from Lehi's camp by the Red Sea?

When Nephi returned with the brass plates, Lehi "did offer sacrifice and burnt offerings unto the Lord." (5:9.) Where did the sacrificial animals come from? Did they have them with them, or were there people nearby from whom they could have purchased animals?

In chapter 7, Nephi and his brothers return for Ishmael's family, and we see the same terminology of going "up" to Jerusalem and "down" to the wilderness. (Vv. 2-5.) How long a wait was there between the time they got the brass plates and the time they made this second trip back?

In chapter 16, they receive the Liahona and "gather together whatsoever things we should carry into the wilderness, and all the remainder of our provisions which the Lord had given unto us" (Were there other provisions than the ones they had brought with them out of Jerusalem?); "and we did take seed of every kind." (V. 11.) Where did they get seed? Did they harvest it? Buy it? Had they brought it with them?

In the next verse we read: ". . . we did take our tents and depart into the wilderness, across the river Laman." (V. 12.) Does this mean that Lehi's camp had been on the west side of the river? Were they now proceeding south on the east side? Then in 16:13 they make a sprint, it seems, for four days in "nearly a south-southeast direction," finally pitching their tents in a camp they called Shazer. Where did they end up after that four-day march?

"And we did go forth again [so they must have stayed there, for a while at least] in the wilderness, following the same direction [this must be south-southeast], keeping in the most fertile parts of the wilderness, which were in the borders near the Red Sea." (V. 14.) What would be the most fertile parts?

And how long did they go this time? Nephi's only answer is "for the space of many days [does that mean a more leisurely but continuous journey?], slaying food by the way, with our bows and our arrows and our stones and our slings" (v. 15) until they needed to rest (v. 17).

Then disaster strikes. In verse 18, Nephi's bow "made of fine steel" breaks and his brothers are upset because "their bows [had] lost their springs." (V. 21.) What would cause a steel bow to break and other bows to lose their springs?

After Nephi makes a new bow and arrow out of wood and hunts for food (What kind of wood could he find in the desert? What kind of animals could he hunt?), they "again take [their] journey, traveling nearly the same course [that's important in determining their direction] . . . for the space of many days." Then, Nephi specifies, "we did pitch our tents again that we might tarry for the space of a time." (Vv. 23, 31, 33.) Where would this have been, and what is "the" space of "a" time? It almost sounds as though there were a defined amount of time involved. Then Ishmael "died, and was buried in the place which was called Nahom." (V. 34.) Called Nahom by whom? Why would they have buried him there? How long would the predeath illness, the burial, and the mourning ceremonies be likely to take?

In chapter 17, they begin traveling again, but now they head "nearly eastward from that time forth." Was that until they reached the end of their journey? "And we did travel and wade through much affliction in the wilderness." (V. 1.) Is there a difference between traveling and wading? What does "much affliction" mean? In verse 2, we discover them living "upon raw meat." Why would they have needed to eat meat without cooking it?

After sojourning eight years in the wilderness (v. 4), "we did come to the land which we called Bountiful, because of its much fruit and also wild honey." Honey implies there were flowers and flowering crops like alfalfa. "And we beheld the sea, which we called Irreantum [this must be different from the Red Sea], which, being interpreted, is many waters." (V. 5.) Was it bigger than the Red Sea? They then pitched their tents "by the seashore." (V. 6.) So there must have been a hospitable beach or at least a meadowlike stretch where they could put their tents and animals. Nephi "went up into the mountain" (Is there only one? It must have been nearby), and inquired of the Lord where to "find ore to molten." (Vv. 7, 9.) Where are there ore deposits that could have been used? He then made "tools of the ore which I did molten out of the rock." (V. 16.) About how long is that process? What kind of tools would he have needed?

Nephi's brothers rebelled because of their hardships, and when Nephi chastised them they became angry and "came forth to lay their hands upon [him] . . . to throw [him] into the depths of the sea." (V. 48.) One can't do that from a sandy beach; it would seem that there must be cliffs at Bountiful.

Thwarted by the power of God, which made them tremble, Nephi's brothers began to cooperate with him in building the ship, which he stresses three times in 18:2 was "not after the manner of men." How did he know what shipbuilding "after the manner of men" was like? How was his different? What was it made of? Where are there trees along the Arabian coast big enough to form ship timbers? Finally, "after we had prepared all things, much fruits and meat from the wilderness, and honey in abundance, and provisions . . . , we did go down into the ship, with all our loading and our seeds." (V. 6.) Seeds again—had they harvested another crop? What provisions would they have been likely to take? How long a voyage was contemplated? Was the land Bountiful relatively small so that it was not an elaborate journey to go hunting in the wilderness?

Forming a Theory

Those are some of the clues that Nephi gives us, and those were some of the questions that came to our minds. So we started thinking, piecing together possible answers to our questions and examining scholars' works, both ancient and modern, for whatever help they could give us.

As we prepared to make our journey, we wrote letters to over one hundred Arab friends in seven Middle East countries, explaining our plans. We were astonished and overwhelmed with gratitude at their enthusiastic responses and offers to help. All seemed anxious that we succeed in our search, for we would be looking in the ancestral homeland of all Arabs, the Saudi Arabian peninsula. These friends, we felt, would be a crucial key to unlocking our understanding of Nephi's words. Our supposition proved true.

But early in our thinking and research an outline or picture of Lehi's trek began to form in our minds, and these ideas were later buttressed by the insights and information graciously shared by our longtime friends and new acquaintances in the Middle East and our own experience. To form that mental outline, a theory really, we drew on the scholarship of Middle East experts in Utah, our own reading in ancient and contemporary accounts of Arabia, and some small but exciting hints from Latter-day Saint history. A central figure was Dr. Hugh Nibley, whose series of ten articles in the *Improvement Era* in 1950 first examined in detail the available scholarly evidence for the accuracy of the Book of Mormon account of Lehi's trip through Arabia. In support of the divine origin of the Book of Mormon, Brother Nibley showed that that evidence had not been available to Joseph Smith and had in fact become well known only in the twentieth century.

Besides his interesting work on such things as the appropriateness to Arab culture of Book of Mormon names and poetic expressions, Dr. Nibley made important suggestions

ALEXANDRIA

JERUSALEM   AMMAN

ON

PETRA   MA`AN

AQABA
Ezion-geber

AL BEDA   TABUK
*Probable Valley
of Lemuel*

AL AZIAN
Probable Shazer

R E D

UMM LAJJ
Leucê Comê

MEDINA

S E A

JIDDAH
*Possible Area of the Camp
of the Broken Bow*

QAL 'AT BISHAH

AL KUNFIDAH
Probable Nahom

ABHA   NAJRAN

SAN`A

A R A

Possible route of Lehi's journey in the wilderness

The Frankincense Trails

The ancient caravan route that is known as the frankincense trail follows almost exactly the theoretical trail constructed from the account recorded in the Book of Mormon. The much traveled trail begins at the coast of modern Oman. From there it goes from ancient waterhole to waterhole throughout the Middle East. We should note that the word *trail* does not refer to a well-defined, narrow path or roadway, but to a more general route that followed a valley or canyon. The width of the route varied with the geography, ranging from a half mile to up to fifty miles wide at one point.

Lehi's Trail

The Book of Mormon does not say that Lehi was hiding on his journey, nor does it say that he was fleeing pursuit, as some have thought. It is likely that he kept to the known highways of the day rather than roamed in the waterless mountains and deserts. Further evidence for this supposition is Nephi's statement that they traveled in the borders of the Red Sea, later south-southeast, and finally eastward, arriving at the land they called Bountiful.

SALALAH
Probable Bountiful

I A N   S E A

As Dr. Nibley suggests, Lehi was apparently like Moses, who spent an early apprenticeship in the desert before the Lord used him to lead the children of Israel across Sinai.

about the route: that Lehi was obviously familiar with desert travel and therefore knew the main caravan routes, and that he most likely followed one of those down the Wadi al 'Araba to the Red Sea at Aqaba, then along the eastern coast to about the nineteenth north latitude, where he would have had to make the turn east reported in 1 Nephi 17 to reach the fertile Qara mountains on the seacoast. This area, which Dr. Nibley pinpointed as the only likely place for Bountiful, was discovered in the 1920s and made known to a surprised world by Bertram Thomas in 1932.

The general route seemed theoretically possible, but was there indeed such a passable trail, perhaps even a caravan route that Lehi could have known about? As Dr. Nibley suggests, Lehi was apparently like Moses, who spent an early apprenticeship in the desert before the Lord used him to lead the children of Israel across Sinai. In the expanded version of his work, *An Approach to the Book of Mormon,*[6] Dr. Nibley showed that Lehi also could have been involved in commercial ventures, such as those that we now know brought some Jews of Lehi's time into extensive dealings with the Arabs, travel along the caravan routes, including protection of local sheikhs, and even permanent colonization. Lehi may well have been chosen for the great work of leading a group of the house of Israel across Arabia on the way to a promised land because his early life so prepared him in the ways of the desert, or possibly the Lord provided him that desert experience in preparing him. Could we find the route along which the Lord, using Lehi's own knowledge and the Liahona, led him?

---

[6]Hugh Nibley, *An Approach to the Book of Mormon* (Salt Lake City: Deseret Book Co, 1964), pp. 47ff.

The Frankincense Trail

Gradually, from our study and thinking, a clearer picture began to emerge. It was especially exciting to learn of an ancient caravan route that followed almost exactly the theoretical trail we had constructed from the Book of Mormon and other Church sources. Known as the "frankincense trail," it originated at the ancient source of frankincense, a fertile spot on the coast of modern Oman that seemed the only place to fit Nephi's description of Bountiful.

We realized that a cursory reading of the Book of Mormon might give the impression that Lehi and his family traveled into a desert vacuum, barren of people and civilization and far from any well-traveled route; yet a more careful reading of the text reveals several clues indicating inhabited regions connected by much-used trails. Lehi could not have traveled without food and water for his family and his beasts of burden. Nephi records no miraculous manna descending to feed them—they had to work hard for their food, and sometimes they complained because of hunger. No waters are reported gushing miraculously from "rocks of Horeb," as Moses had produced with the touch of his rod. The family, therefore, must have traveled and survived as other travelers of their day did in the same area, going from public waterhole to public waterhole. (Of course, they also had the heaven-sent Liahona to help them find watering places along any route the Lord may have chosen, but the human-made wells so important in crossing the worst desert areas would have been only along established routes like the frankincense trail.) As we traveled through the Middle East, we never saw a fresh water source devoid of people; where water is so precious, it is unlikely that many waterholes are unknown.

One campsite was almost certainly a settled place, because Nephi says it already "was called Nahom," while every other named campsite—the Valley of Lemuel, the camp at Shazer, the land Bountiful—was named by the people themselves. Of course, these places might also have been common oases that were simply renamed by Lehi's family. It is the habit of Semitic people to name even already-known things after their personal experience; and because these places had such great meaning to the Lehi group, Lehi apparently gave them private names known to all persons in his family to help implant his teachings.

Nephi periodically tells us that the group offered animal sacrifices. Where did these animals come from? To take goat and sheep flocks, which wander all over the landscape in search of forage, would have slowed their journey to a snail's pace,

"...he shall prepare a way"

Concerning the presence of other peoples, there can be no doubt that nomadic Bedouin tribes occupied the Arabian peninsula from ancient times. For example, Jethro, "the priest of Midian" and father-in-law of Moses, lived as a Bedouin in the land of Midian. This area in northwest Saudi Arabia, through which Lehi probably journeyed, had a vast livestock population: the armies of Israel, after conquering Midian, took as booty 675,000 sheep plus much other treasure.

and unlike camels, goats and sheep require water every day. However, Lehi could have purchased or traded for these animals from local Bedouin herders and still have traveled at normal caravan speed.

Concerning the presence of other peoples, there can be no doubt that nomadic Bedouin tribes occupied the Arabian peninsula from ancient times. For example, Jethro, "the priest of Midian" and father-in-law of Moses, lived as a Bedouin in the land of Midian. (Exodus 2:16, 3:1.) This area in northwest Saudi Arabia, through which Lehi probably journeyed, had a vast livestock population: the armies of Israel, after conquering Midian, took as booty 675,000 sheep plus much other treasure. (Numbers 31:43.)

Another evidence of inhabited regions along Lehi's route is that when Nephi began to build his ship he specified that he did not "build the ship after the manner of men." (1 Nephi 18:2.) Could he have written such a statement if he had not seen ships—in fact, seen them being built? It was eye-opening to us to discover that all along the coast of the Red Sea are shipbuilding villages where the ancient art has been practiced for generations upon generations.

Ancient Testimony
That there were villages and a well-established civilization in the barren wilderness along the Red Sea shore within six hundred years of Lehi's day is verified by two eye-witness records.

Using firsthand accounts, Strabo, a Greek historian, wrote of the ill-fated Roman army of 10,000 infantrymen that left Egypt in 24 B.C. under Aelius Gallus to capture the "incense country" in southern Arabia. The soldiers traveled much of what we believe is the trail Lehi used, confirming that many people lived along the route; that the route itself was important and well known, extending north from where the army landed in Arabia at Leucê Comê to Petra in Jordan as well as south to the incense country; that the journey was difficult (the majority of the soldiers died of starvation, thirst, and illness, although primarily due to the treachery of their disloyal guide); and that they had to carry water on camels and buy their provisions from the Arab "hucksters and merchants."[1]

An unknown Greek author wrote a travelogue called *The Periplus of the Erythraean Sea* around A.D. 57. He sailed around

[1]Strabo of Amasia, *The Geography of Strabo*, trans. Horace Leonard Jones (London: William Heinemann Ltd., 1930), 7:353-63. See Appendix II.

the Arabian peninsula, touching at many ports that fall along Lehi's probable route. This volume gives an eye-witness verification that during the first century of any outside influence that might have begun to change the culture there were many long-established villages and markets, a heavy traffic in frankincense from Oman, and extensive shipping—and also regular monsoon winds at a critical point on the route.[2]

An even earlier account—but not firsthand—comes from the Greek historian Herodotus, who lived from 485 to 430 B.C. and wrote within 150 years of Lehi's time. He said that "Arabia is the farthest of inhabited countries towards the south; and this is the only region in which grow frankincense [and] myrrh."[3] He also reported on the distance of eastern Arabia from Memphis: "I have heard that it is a two months' journey from east to west; and that westward its confines produce frankincense."[4] He said that Arabians rode camels, which are "not inferior to horses in swiftness, and are much better able to carry burdens."[5]

Thus, it was a major discovery for us to find that both modern and ancient maps of the area show that among the most heavily traveled roads of the ancient world were the generally well-known frankincense trails. One ran along the Red Sea coast about three-quarters of the length of the Arabian peninsula, then turned eastward. At Najran it again turned south into Yemen. The second route roughly paralleled the first a hundred or more miles inland, intersecting the coastal route at Najran. This route, however, turned eastward from Najran to Salalah. These routes were in common use at least nine hundred years before Lehi's day and likely even hundreds of years before that.[6] Evidence of both these roads is ample even today. Both routes are easy to follow from the crumbling ruins of strategically placed stone forts built in the tenth century B.C. by the Sabaean civilization, then added to by the Nabateans and later by the Romans as they sought to protect the passing caravans. These forts were also used as taxing points for the kingdoms through which the trails passed.

Following page: This *siq* (narrow gorge) is the only entrance to Petra, fabled ancient city in the northern part of the Arabian desert midway between the south tip of the Dead Sea and the Gulf of Aqaba. The elaborate facade, chiseled into the rock itself, towers 90 feet high.

[2]Wilfred H. Schoff, trans., *The Periplus of the Erythraean Sea* (New Delhi: Oriental Books Reprint Corp., 1974). See Appendix III.
[3]Henry Cary, trans., *Herodotus* (London: George Bell and Sons, 1891), p. 215.
[4]Ibid., p. 97.
[5]Ibid., p. 214.
[6]See *The Periplus*, pp. 120-21.

As for the major purpose of the trail, the frankincense trade was heavy as well as lucrative. Some idea of the extent of this traffic can be seen from the fact that anciently five sizable Arab kingdoms in the southwest corner of Arabia—Saba (Sheba), Qataban, Hadramaut, Ma'in and Ausan—were supported in high style by it. Three hundred years before Lehi, King Solomon received spices from the Queen of Sheba. Both Isaiah and Jeremiah speak of incense coming from Sheba, and Isaiah assures us that the Arabs of Midian, the area east of the Gulf of Aqaba, were caravanners and possessed a "multitude of camels." The Old Testament also reports that in the days of the judges these same Midianites had "camels ... without number, as the sand by the sea side for multitude." Travel up and down the 2,100-mile frankincense trail was the heaviest in Lehi's very era.

Also, from Petra in Jordan to Najran in southern Saudi Arabia the trail route is easily identified by the desert graffiti carved by thousands of camel drivers in the flat stones of the hills on both sides of the route. These traders plied their monotonous way northward leading heavily laden camels whose precious cargo of frankincense fed the insatiable needs of the temples in Jerusalem, Egypt, and Babylon.

The Trail

We should note that the word *trail* is apt to be misleading. It does not refer to a well-defined, relatively narrow path or roadway, but to a more general route that followed through this valley, that canyon, etc. The width of the route varied with the geography, ranging from a half mile to a dozen (even at one point up to fifty) miles wide. Travelers could thus camp great distances from one another and still be at the same point on the same trail.

As for the major purpose of the trail, the frankincense trade was heavy as well as lucrative. Some idea of the extent of this traffic can be seen from the fact that anciently five sizable Arab kingdoms in the southwest corner of Arabia—Saba (Sheba), Qataban, Hadramaut, Ma'in and Ausan[7]—were supported in high style by it. Three hundred years before Lehi, King Solomon received spices from the Queen of Sheba. (2 Chronicles 9:1.) Both Isaiah and Jeremiah speak of incense coming from Sheba (see Isaiah 60:6 and Jeremiah 6:20), and Isaiah assures us that the Arabs of Midian, the area east of the Gulf of Aqaba, were caravanners and possessed a "multitude of camels" (Isaiah 60:6). The Old Testament also reports that in the days of the judges these same Midianites had "camels ... without number, as the sand by the sea side for multitude." (Judges 7:12.) Travel up and down the 2,100-mile frankincense trail was the heaviest in Lehi's very era.[8]

Thus, we found that there existed a well-traveled, south-southeastern route along the Red Sea coast. We believe that Lehi would not have left an established path to roam on waterless mountains and deserts. The Book of Mormon does not say he was hiding on his journey, nor does it say he was fleeing pursuit as some have thought; so it is likely that he kept to the known highways of the day. Further evidence for this supposition is Nephi's statement that they traveled in the borders of the Red Sea (1 Nephi 2:5), right where the

[7]Van Beek, p. 41.
[8]Ibid., pp. 36-44.

frankincense trail has existed from ancient times.

Furthermore, such trails were designed to follow the line of oases or ancient wells. On a modern map of the route, drawn by the Saudi Arabian Ministry of Natural Resources, there are 118 waterholes at an average distance of thirty kilometers (eighteen miles) from each other. Lehi could not have carved out a route for himself without water, and for a city dweller to discover a line of waterholes of which desert-dwellers were ignorant is an unlikely prospect, nor does the text suggest that the Lord took them to undiscovered water. Actually, it is likely that once Lehi and his family were on the trail, they met many strangers along the way, most of them not Israelites. We discovered that Arabs were the main caravanners of Lehi's time, and the Sabataeans from San'a (now Yemen's capital) may have been frequent visitors in Lehi's tent and he in theirs.

Frankincense

Thus, as a result of our pretrip studies, we felt that we had found a probable route southward for Lehi's family. But its existence raised more questions. Why was frankincense so valuable? Authors have recorded great caravans of camels heading northward bearing 225 kilos (500 pounds) apiece.[9] We turned to the Bible for clues and found that when Jehovah commanded the ancient Israelites, through Moses, to use incense in worshiping him, he gave them a formula for compounding it: equal parts of stacte, onycha, galbanum, and pure frankincense. This mixture was sacred and could not be used for other purposes nor burned by any unauthorized person. (See Exodus 30:7-9; 34-38; Leviticus 10:1-7.) It was especially symbolic of prayer ascending to God (see Psalm 141:2; Revelation 8:3-5) and originally was burned near the veil that concealed the Holy of Holies. It may also have been used as a deodorizer against the smells of the slaughtering and burning of sacrificial animals. On the Day of Atonement frankincense was burned within the Holy of Holies so that the mercy seat was "enveloped in a cloud of fragrant smoke."[10] Further study showed that Jews were not alone in combining worship with frankincense; it was "common in the religious ceremonies of nearly all ancient nations (Egyptians, Babylonians, Assyrians, Phoenicians, etc.)."[11] Early Christians over six hundred years after Lehi's day also felt that frankincense symbolically carried

---

[9]Ibid., pp. 40-41.
[10]Merrill C. Tenney, ed., *The Zondervan Pictorial Bible Dictionary* (Grand Rapids, Mich.: Zondervan House, 1963), pp. 373-74.
[11]Ibid.

prayers heavenward, and the walls of early churches are blackened from burning incense.

It was also customary in classical times to burn frankincense in the funeral pyre. Pliny the Elder, a prolific Roman writer of the first century A.D., relates that on one occasion the entire year's production of Arabian frankincense was burned in the funeral pyre of Poppaea, the wife of the Emperor Nero.[12]

We knew now why frankincense was in such great demand. But why was it so costly, and where did it come from? Frankincense is the dried, creamy-yellow gum of the frankincense tree, indigenous to a tiny sickle-shaped area at the bottom of the Arabian peninsula. This place, now called Salalah, is situated on the coast of the Arabian Sea in the state of Dhofar in the Sultanate of Oman. The trees there are "milked" twice yearly. The resulting sticky gum, with its strong, spicy aroma, can be chewed or burned. Today Arabian children do chew it, for it costs little more than chewing gum, even though in biblical times frankincense and myrrh ranked with gold as gifts suitable for the Christ child. (See Matthew 2:11.)

Lehi and the Desert

This information raised several questions in our minds. Obviously, Lehi was man of considerable wealth. The casual catalogue of "gold, and . . . silver, and . . . precious things" that Nephi makes indicates a better than average income. (1 Nephi 2:4.) Salim Saad, one of our friends in Amman, Jordan, pointed out that Jerusalem, like Mecca later, would most likely have already been a tourist town, flooded by pilgrims on holy days. Consequently, its inhabitants would have been mostly innkeepers, priests, garrison soldiers, and specialized merchants, with a sprinkling of those who transported goods into the city. This last occupation suggests another way that Lehi could have been one who had some business with the desert.

On the other hand, the foremost archaeologist of southern Arabia for the past decade, Gus W. Van Beek, cites archaeological evidence that the flourishing Arab kingdoms of the Yemen in the first millennium B.C. controlled the caravan trade routes all the way from Oman to Egypt, Damascus, and Baghdad.[13] The Bible reports that a caravan of Ishmaelites bought Joseph, son of Jacob, as a slave and took him to Egypt. (Genesis 37:25-28.) Nowhere do we learn that the children of Israel were prominent in the caravan business. It is always

[12]Van Beek, p. 40
[13]Ibid., pp. 36-39.

Arabs. The Bible mentions only occasional journeys for a special purpose by Israelites, as when Abraham's servant took a caravan to Haran to obtain a wife for Isaac (Genesis 24) or when the eleven sons of Jacob went to Egypt for corn (Genesis 42:3). But it is well known that these accounts of occasional desert travel do not constitute participation in the caravan trade.

Yet Lehi had tents at a time when making them was a laborious and time-consuming process of weaving out of durable goats hair. And according to Salim Saad, who among many other things is an eminent historian, travelers in Judea generally camped in caves; tents were for desert travelers. Why would a city dweller have tents in his possession, ready when he wanted to leave?

Salim, familiar with the Book of Mormon, speculated that Lehi may have lived on the "lands of his inheritance," which perhaps were a number of miles outside of Jerusalem. On these lands he could have raised goats, sheep, fruits, and grains, with which he supplied one of the markets, or *suqs*, in the old, walled city of Jerusalem. Another possibility is that Lehi's real wealth may have been made in conjunction with some business that took him into the desert frequently, such as buying supplies for Jerusalem markets from Arab caravans in the desert south of Jerusalem.

All of this is speculative, of course; but if Lehi had some type of dealing with desert people, it might explain several things: (1) why he apparently had sufficient tents and animals to move his family without making extraordinary preparations; (2) why his sons knew how to handle tents and travel in the wilderness; and (3) how he had sufficient knowledge of the main routes and waterholes to survive prior to receiving the Liahona.

Out of Jerusalem

We are on slightly firmer ground when we talk about how Lehi actually left the area of Jerusalem. It is almost certain that the chief beast of burden in Jerusalem and the Judean hill country was the donkey, better fitted than the camel to negotiate the rocky paths and the twisting alleys of the city, with its overhanging arches and balconies. One of the reasons that the camel trade bypassed Jerusalem (traders from Jerusalem went out to meet the caravans as they passed to the east) was because the soil there is rocky, with sharp flints that would have slashed the camel's large, unhooved, cushionlike foot. By going along the sandy road of the western coast and the relatively smooth

Lehi had tents at a time when making them was a laborious and time-consuming process of weaving out of durable goats hair. And according to Salim Saad, who among many other things is an eminent historian, travelers in Judea generally camped in caves; tents were for desert travelers. Why would a city dweller have tents in his possession, ready when he wanted to leave?

Preceding page: The King's Highway as it appears in the land of Moab. This north-south road is one of three possible routes out of Jerusalem that Lehi and his family took when they left the city. It is more probable, however, that they went down the west side of the Dead Sea, not the east side where this highway was located.

King's Highway, an extremely ancient road that runs east of the Jordan River from Syria to the Gulf of Aqaba, the camel caravans continued north.[14]

We discovered that there are three routes out of Jerusalem, each of which would have taken Lehi to the city of Aqaba at the head of the Red Sea. One route went east from Jerusalem to Jericho through the bleak Judean wilderness, then crossed the Jordan River and joined the King's Highway, going down the east bank of the Dead Sea through the towns of Madaba, Karak, and Petra to Aqaba, all of which are in the present-day Hashemite Kingdom of Jordan. This is the main ancient north-south road, winding up mountains and over wadis. (Wadis are sandfilled washes or valleys between mountains that receive the rain runoff from the steep mountains around them. Thus, during the rainy season they can be dangerous, muddy torrents. But during the dry season, they are sand-cushioned "superhighways" with gently sloping gradients and comfortable passageways through the rough and otherwise impenetrable hills.) This route was well known even 800 years before Lehi when Moses mentioned it in asking permission to proceed along it without turning "to the right hand nor to the left" with the hosts of Israel on their way to Canaan. (Numbers 20:17, 21:22.) However, Lehi would have had to pass through the kingdoms of Ammon, Moab, and Edom on this eastern route; and even though the family might not have been in any danger, they would almost certainly have been taxed at each border.

Another possible route leaves Jerusalem and goes south to Hebron, continues southwest to Beersheba, then goes down Wadi al 'Araba to Aqaba. A variation of this route turns east at Hebron and crosses Salt Mountain on a trail that is still just a footpath, descends a steep slope, and emerges on the west shore of the Dead Sea just below the oasis of En-gedi, joining at that point another possible route that will be described next. This route seems to be an unusually complicated and difficult alternative.

The third route goes east from Jerusalem on the same road as the first route, turning south just before Jericho, passing the Dead Sea on the west, continuing past the caves and cliffs of Qumran, and then through the Wadi Al 'Araba to emerge at Aqaba. Our friends in the Middle East, knowledgeable in the history of their past, told us that this latter route is the most probable.

---

[14]J. D. Douglas, ed., "King's Highway," *The New Bible Dictionary* (Grand Rapids, Mich.: William B. Eerdmans Publishing Co., 1973), p. 700.

But no matter which route Lehi took to leave Jerusalem, all three routes converge south of the Dea Sea in the Wadi al 'Araba, which leads to Aqaba at the head of the Red Sea on the Gulf of Aqaba. To be in Aqaba must have been great education for young Nephi, because it was a center for metal smelting and shipbuilding, both of which industries later became useful to him when he built the ship to take his people to America.

Aqaba, formerly called Ezion-geber, was the chief city of the ancient desert kingdom of Edom. Over three hundred years before Lehi's family had left Jerusalem, King David had captured Edom. (2 Samuel 8:14.) Israel had begun smelting copper and iron ores there, and King Solomon greatly added to his wealth and power by exploiting this natural resource. He stationed his navy in Aqaba (1 Kings 9:26), and later Jehoshaphat of Judah built another fleet there (1 Kings 22:48). Aqaba is situated on the only way between Jerusalem and the ancient Red Sea coast road, the intersection of civilization and the wilderness in that ancient world.

*South-southeast
and East*

Where would Lehi have gone from Aqaba? The entire Arabian peninsula lay before him, of course, but it is the well-traveled frankincense trail that runs south-southeasterly along the Arabian Red Sea coastline, with 118 known water wells spread along its trail.

However, as the frankincense trail moves into the lower quarter of the Arabian peninsula, it turns eastward. In fact, various forks break eastward and cut up through the mountains, then join near Abha. The trail continues eastward before branching at Najran, the main branch going south to present-day San'a, capital of Yemen, and the other lesser-used branch cutting across more than half of the lower portion of the Arabian peninsula before ending at the Qara mountains.

Since the Red Sea does not run directly north and south, Lehi's party would have been coming "nearly . . . south-southeast" (1 Nephi 16:13) as they paralleled its coast. After Ishmael's burial at Nahom, they turned "nearly eastward" (1 Nephi 17:1) until they came to many waters. Since it appears to us that Lehi was on the frankincense trail on the way down the Red Sea coast, and since it also appears that he was on the frankincense trail as he crossed the peninsula and arrived at the trail's natural end, it also appears that the locale of Nahom would be in the area where the frankincense trail is known to have turned eastward. Thus, we determined that a study of the communities in this area might uncover a possible Nahom.

After Lehi and his party had turned east, they continued nearly eastward until they came to Irreantum, the "many waters" upon which they later embarked. At this point in our study, an item from Church history was interesting. The Prophet Joseph Smith is quoted as saying that "Lehi went down by the Red Sea to the great Southern Ocean, and crossed over to this land," meaning America.[15] What would the "great Southern Ocean" have been but the Arabian Sea and Indian Ocean to the south of Arabia? Thus, Nephi's care in specifying *nearly* south-southeast and then *nearly* east allowed us to make a likely speculation about the location of their destination and next major stop, the land Bountiful.

The End of the Trail

As Nephi described the land Bountiful, it must have contained water, fruit, large trees for a ship, grass, wild honeybees, flowers or blossoms, a mountain, a shoreline, a cliff overlooking the depths of the sea, and metal ore. Incredible as it seems, the south coast of the Arabian peninsula from Perim to Sur has such a place, the *only one place* in its entire length of 1,400 miles that meets that description—and it is at one end of the frankincense trail! It is the modern Salalah, curved around a little bay, about twenty-eight miles long and only seven miles wide, and backed by the Qara Mountains. For the three months of the summer, monsoon clouds gather on the slopes fronting the sea and cover them with fog, mist, and rain. The coast in both directions stretches away in unbroken barrenness. We repeat, this is the *only* place on the whole Arabian peninsula seashore that receives significant rainfall and where large trees grow—and it is now known to have been this way for well over two thousand years.

Our enthusiasm mounted as we read together descriptions of the place. British explorer Wilfred Thesiger, who had visited Salalah in 1948, said: "The jungle trees are wreathed with jasmine and giant convolvulus and roped together with lianas. Massive tamarinds grow in the valleys, and on the downs great fig-trees rise above the wind-rippled grass like oaks in an English park."[16] (Lynn had, coincidentally, been

[15]Joseph Fielding Smith, comp., *Teachings of the Prophet Joseph Smith* (Salt Lake City: Deseret Book Co., rev. and enlarged, 1976), p. 267.
[16]Wilfred Thesiger, *Arabian Sands* (Middlesex, England: Penguin Books Ltd., 1964), p. 47.

reading Thesiger's book in Egypt and wondering if Salalah were Bountiful only a few weeks before Jay Todd called us.)

We next discovered the reason for its ancient traffic: Salalah is the only place on earth where frankincense trees are indigenous. Seedlings have been transplanted to Yemen and Somaliland on the African coast, but at the time of Lehi, Salalah held a near monopoly.[17] Pliny, a Greek naturalist (A.D. 23-79), described the land of frankincense bounded by the sea and by high cliffs. (See Appendix D.) He said that only 3,000 families were even allowed to see the trees; during pruning and harvest such supposedly polluting factors as women or dead bodies were strictly excluded from the area.[18] *The Periplus,* which recounts the voyage of a Greek merchant of the first century A.D., tells fantastic stories of poisonous serpents that guarded the trees and had to be pacified by the smoke of a cheaper incense called styrax.[19]

To say we were excited to learn of these statements is to put it mildly. Wasn't it almost certain that Salalah, the beginning point of the frankincense trails and the only place on the southern Arabian coast where there was enough timber to build a boat, was indeed the land Bountiful?

Thus our research ended. The route and the chronology as we pieced it together had Lehi joining one of the most heavily traveled routes of antiquity, the frankincense trail originating in Salalah, Oman. For us, this explains the presence of named water sources, the direction the group traveled, and the people they undoubtedly met.

Now we were ready to test the hypothesis by driving over the ground, checking distances, seeing for ourselves the existence of the frankincense trail, and examining this centuries-old area, which fit so well the description of Bountiful. We were ready for Arabia!

A Window Opens
"A window opens sometimes only a few inches and we need to take advantage of the light." How prophetic were the words spoken to us in an interview before our departure by Elder Robert D. Hales, Assistant to the Council of the Twelve! But as we left Salt Lake City on a cold day in January 1976, snow flanking the roadside as we drove toward the airport, it seemed that all windows had suddenly closed, for we were leaving the United States without the required entry permits for the

Salalah is the only place on the whole Arabian peninsula that receives enough rainfall to grow trees large enough to build a ship such as Nephi would have needed. It is now known to have been this way for well over two thousand years.

[17]Van Beek, pp. 36, 41.
[18]Pliny, *Natural History,* trans. H. Rackham (London: William Heinemann Ltd., 1952), 4:39.
[19]*The Periplus,* pp. 131-32.

countries of Oman and Saudi Arabia. To minimize entry difficulties in the four countries we needed to pass through, we were advised to visit the Arab countries first and end up in Jerusalem, thus tracing Lehi's trail in reverse, but we had been denied visas. Personal trips to the embassies in Washington, D.C., letters, and in the final weeks urgent telephone calls and telegrams couched in pleading terms had all proved useless.

When we applied, neither Oman nor Saudi Arabia, busy with rapid development projects for their people, had been taking time for tourist travelers; therefore they had not been issuing tourist visas. Visitors to these countries had to be sponsored by a business company or an individual living within the country. As we scanned our list of Arab friends we found none living in Oman; in fact, all replied to our inquiries that they had never been to Oman nor did they know anyone who lived there. And we knew Omani officials would be especially reluctant to admit visitors because of a dangerous guerilla war that was still in progress.

In Cairo, Egypt, Lynn received a thirty-day businessman's entry visa to Saudi Arabia because he operates a water-well drilling business in Egypt. The rest of us did not have such good fortune and Oman again flatly rejected visa requests for any of us. Because of lack of hotel rooms we stayed for two days with our good friend Angie Chukri in her apartment in a newly completed five-story apartment house in Heliopolis, a Cairo suburb. It was here that the decision was made to proceed to Oman, turning back if the way were barred by government officials.

As we carried our heavy bags full of cameras and equipment down the five flights of stairs in the predawn darkness, we whispered to Miss Angie that we would likely return in a couple of hours when we were not allowed to board the airplane to Muscat, Oman. It was 4:30 A.M., dark and cold on a Saturday morning. We wondered how long we'd have to wait for two taxis: with four people and eight suitcases we could not fit into one of the small Fiats that dart in and out of the overcrowded Cairo streets. Mohammed, Angie's doorman, preceded us onto the dusty street in front of the house toward the main paved road, his thin form almost lost under three of our huge suitcases. As he approached the street he dropped the suitcases and began waving his arms wildly; he had spotted an oncoming taxi far down the road. Seconds later it loomed into our view, and we saw that not only had we found a taxi, but it was also a large Mercedes. We climbed in to the lilt of Lynn's words that "this is a good omen for Oman." For a moment his humor relaxed our tense feelings.

At the Cairo International Airport, a man at the Middle East Airlines counter was checking tickets and handing out boarding passes. Hope was assigned the job of taking the four passports and, with as large a smile as she could nervously muster, presenting them to the agent. Barely daring to breathe for fear we would be turned back, we felt that seconds passed like minutes, until the agent cheerfully gave us the passports with four boarding passes. Our itinerary indicated that an overnight stop in Bahrein was necessary, and our U.S. travel agent had told us there was no connecting flight that same day to Oman. Bahrein, an island in the Arabian Gulf, appears so flat from the air that we wondered what kept it from complete inundation from a one-foot wave. It was sultry and hot as we landed, and our heavy coats and sweaters worn in cold Cairo made us miserable. We hurried to shed extra clothing, while Hope began trying to make hotel reservations for an overnight stay in Bahrein.

The young woman at the counter at Middle East Airlines, seeing Lynn's ticket, asked, "Would you like to fly on to Oman right now?" It seems the plane scheduled to fly to Oman had been delayed thirty minutes. "Let me see if there are four empty seats on the flight," she continued, and we held our breath again. There *were* just four seats on the late airplane—another good omen for Oman.

More than half of the passengers on the plane disembarked en route at the postage-stamp-sized country of Dubai, and minutes later we were airborne again, needing only the cooperation of the officials at Seeb International Airport, thirty miles south of Muscat. Inside the airport two lines had already formed when we arrived, one before a sign marked "Omani Nationals," and the other in front of "Passengers with Visas." We selected the second line and prayed.

The airport officials confined us to a room in the airport, without access to our luggage, for seven hours, and we began to think we were to be deported, as was another man on our same flight. Finally, however, we were granted permission to go into Muscat overnight without passports, with instructions to meet the immigration officer the following morning. But we were actually in Muscat, Oman, in a beautiful hotel. Surely this good fortune meant the window was opening.

The next day we went with much trepidation to see the immigration officer. To our surprise, after we became acquainted, he allowed his clerk to put a six-day visa stamp on our passports! In addition, we were able to obtain visas for Saudi Arabia in that country's embassy in Oman. Now our problem was how to reach Salalah. Only one flight per day left for this remote area, and special government permission was required because of guerilla fighting in that area.

We spent a day exploring and photographing in and around Muscat, in constant fear that this was the closest we would get to Salalah, and considering which government agency might logically help us. After another night of prayerful consideration, we felt impressed to try the Minister of Information, whose office we had noticed in our travels. A young man fluent in English, he was in charge of all government programs related to public information. We showed him the hypothetical map of the Lehi trail that Dr. Nibley had constructed and explained that as historians we were interested in seeing the "big trees" at Salalah. We had come all the way from America for this very purpose, since we had an ancient book that reported that a Semite family built a ship 2,500 years ago, perhaps in Salalah, of the same type of trees, then sailed to America, where their descendants became the American Indians. He was astonished. "Salalah is my home," he said, "and there are large trees there, but I have never heard this story." He agreed to give us passes into the war zone if we would bring letters of introduction from the United States Embassy in Muscat. The U.S. information officer, after hearing our story, gave us the desired letters. Because of the six-day visa granted to us earlier, we then had twenty-four hours to spend in Salalah.

We discovered later that on the very day before our arrival at Muscat the commander of the rebel forces had surrendered to the Sultan of Oman, thus ending thirteen years of hostilities. This was a crucial factor that made it possible, only seven days after our departure from Salt Lake City, for us to be standing on the beautiful white sand beach at Salalah, at one end of the frankincense trail, which we believed Lehi had used. We were looking out upon "Irreantum," the sea of many waters, and contemplating this fertile area, truly a beautiful enclave nestled in the ringed palm of the Qara Mountains. A window had opened wide, and we rejoiced to view what Nephi may have seen 2,500 years ago.

Lehi Leaves Jerusalem

We had only five weeks to spend in the Middle East on our search for Lehi's trail. That was another reason (besides comfort) for choosing an air-conditioned automobile over camels or donkeys for our transportation. Paved highways now cover much of the route, locked onto the ancient frankincense trails by the dictates of wells and topography. Our hardships along the trail included four flat tires in four days (which our Saudi driver, Mohammed Said Salim of Jiddah, fixed easily), and sleeping out one night in Yenbo under the cold January stars. Even then we lay warm in American sleeping bags on *Haj* beds, woven hemp stretched over three-foot-high wooden frames, used by Islamic pilgrims.

Extraordinary cooperation from various Arab officials made it possible for us to make an exciting personal inspection of Salalah, which we believe is the site of Lehi's Bountiful, and to travel over crucial parts of the frankincense trail we believe Lehi followed through Saudi Arabia. But uncertain military conditions made it impossible for us to visit two areas: a stretch in Saudi Arabia along the Red Sea, where we believe Lehi journeyed between the Valley of Lemuel and Shazer, and the desert stretch from Abha east to the Arabian Sea, which we believe was Lehi's route to the land Bountiful. We flew over parts of the latter section and felt satisfied we had covered the route that might most reasonably be construed as Lehi's trail. Although we traveled the route in reverse, we shall present our findings in the order Lehi would have encountered them, beginning with Jerusalem.

We are very much aware that our conclusions about Lehi's experiences and life-style in the desert are accurate only to the extent that the Bedouin life we observed still resembles that of the Bedouins' ancestors 2,600 years ago. Ancient and modern historians corroborate the word of Bedouins themselves that once a custom that enhanced survival had been established, there was little reason to change it and a great deal of reason not to. But, though what we saw was most helpful and illuminating, it cannot be taken as proven fact without a great deal of supplementary research in archaeology, anthropology, and linguistics.

Since Lehi had two married daughters, he was probably over forty-five when he left Jerusalem in 600 B.C., and was therefore approximately thirty-five when his native land, Judah, lost its political independence. He lived during the waning years of the former glory of David's united kingdom, born a citizen of the southern part of the divided monarchy. His

"...take your family and depart into the wilderness"

Jerusalem was a mighty fortress. Lehi's sons Laman and Lemuel felt the city was indestructible, as did many of the sophisticated inhabitants of the city, and, as events proved, and unfortunately for its citizens, it almost *was* indestructible. After King Zedekiah had broken his oath of fealty to Babylon and sided with Egypt, Nebuchadnezzar came and destroyed Jerusalem, but only after a two-year siege. Lehi's timely departure ten years before this time spared him this terrible carnage. The Jews finally surrendered after being driven to cannibalism.

kinsmen in the northern kingdom had long since (721 B.C.) been carried away captive by the Assyrians. Now his own king, Josiah, was killed in a futile war at Megiddo against Egypt's pharaoh, Necho.

Actually, Judah was a small pawn in the larger scheme of events, as the two rival seventh century B.C. powers, Egypt and Babylon, struggled to dominate the area. Lehi had been a witness to the sweeping religious reforms instituted by King Josiah after finding in the temple a copy of Moses' book of the law, probably the Book of Deuteronomy. But these reforms were only temporary, and as Lehi's family was growing up in Jerusalem, he began to proclaim loudly against the abominations he saw in Jerusalem.

Lehi lived to see a series of military defeats. Daniel and the flower of Judah's youth were taken to Babylon in what proved to be the first of three deportations of Jews to Babylon. No doubt sick at heart, and knowing the calamity that awaited his peers, Lehi continued to proclaim repentance, but to no avail.

Josiah's successor on the Jewish throne, Jehoiakim, reverted to the old religious abominations. Lehi witnessed the return of Nebuchadnezzar's Babylonian army and saw 10,000 of his countrymen, including the prophet Ezekiel, carried into captivity. The conqueror Nebuchadnezzar carefully selected the twenty-one-year-old Mattaniah, renamed him Zedekiah, swore him to a role of vassalage, and then, placing him on the throne of Judah, departed. The city remained, but the national power continued under the foreign power of the Chaldeans from Babylon.

At this point, Lehi received the commandment from the Lord to depart for a promised land far away. What a profound decision! Mighty nations yet unborn would flower in a new land because of Lehi's acceptance of the Lord's command. Not knowing beforehand where he would go, he made hasty preparations, for the Jews now sought his life.

Jerusalem was a mighty fortress. Lehi's sons Laman and Lemuel felt the city was indestructible, as did many of the sophisticated inhabitants of the city, and, as events proved, and unfortunately for its citizens, it almost *was* indestructible. After King Zedekiah had broken his oath of fealty to Babylon and sided with Egypt, Nebuchadnezzar came and destroyed Jerusalem, but only after a two-year siege. Lehi's timely departure ten years before this time spared him this terrible carnage. The Jews finally surrendered after being driven to cannibalism.

The Long Journey

As we thought about Lehi's escape from the doomed city, we wondered about the time it took him to make the great journey to which he had been called by the Lord. From Jerusalem to Salalah is 2,102 miles. How fast do camels move? Donkeys? Here we relied on the assistance of Salim Saad, an experienced camel rider and a former British Army officer. Stationed in the Wadi al 'Araba, he had become friends with many desert Bedouins. He explained that a loaded donkey caravan can travel twenty miles in six hours. Drawing on his astonishing library of Arab history, he showed us an example of a camel caravan consisting of thousands of camels averaging twenty-four miles a day on the *Haj* (Islamic pilgrimage) from Cairo to Mecca. The famous archaeologist Nelson Glueck, a novice camel rider, reported he personally averaged thirteen miles a day on a camel ride from Jerusalem to Aqaba. Pliny tells of a journey from Timna in Yemen to Gaza on the Mediterranean Sea coast in Palestine that required "sixty-five stages," which presumably meant sixty-five days on the road.[1] From Timna to Gaza is a distance of 1,534 miles, an average of twenty-four miles per day.

Another measure was provided when the patriarch Jacob in the Bible fled with his sons and wives on camels with his cattle from Padanaram (Haran in Mesopotamia) to Mount Gilead, a distance of approximately 378 miles, in ten days (Genesis 31:18-23)—an average of thirty-eight miles per day. He was overtaken by his irate father-in-law, Laban, who covered the same distance in seven days, or fifty-four miles per day! If we consider all these figures in computing an average, we can assume that Lehi's party could have traveled about twenty-four miles a day, regardless of the type of animals they used. In other words, they could have come from Jerusalem to Salalah in approximately ninety days. Yet Nephi reports that it took the party eight years to reach Bountiful. (1 Nephi 17:4.)

If we start at the beginning and review the record, we can first assume that the group didn't dawdle getting out of Jerusalem and that they probably could have traveled at least as fast as Nelson Glueck (thirteen miles a day). That means eight to twelve days between Jerusalem and Aqaba. From there, they journeyed "three days in the wilderness" and camped in the Valley of Lemuel. (1 Nephi 2:6.) Upon examining the maps and traveling through the area, we decided that there is one oasis that could best qualify as this important campsite—Al Beda in the Wadi El Afal, Saudi

When they left Jerusalem, Lehi and his family probably used donkeys. The land around the city is very sharp and rocky; consequently, very few camels, with their soft padded feet, are in evidence. After Lehi and his family reached the desert, they probably switched their burdens to the more common form of desert transportation. The unique qualities of the camel not only allow it to survive, but also to thrive under harsh desert conditions. To the Arabs the camel is more than the "ship of the desert." It represents a way of life, a special gift from God, a source of food, clothing, shelter, and transportation.

[1]Van Beek, p. 41.

Arabia. Here they may have stayed for as long as two or three very busy years, which would have included twice sending the sons back to Jerusalem on errands, with traveling time of a month each trip, plus the time needed to prepare for and recuperate from the journeys and the days spent haggling with Laban and collecting their gold and silver. There followed long days of studying and digesting the teachings of the brass plates. (How long would it take you to read thoroughly most of the Old Testament and carefully think out its teachings, then present them to your family?) And when Ishmael and his family joined them, there would have been the preparations for the five weddings, with the celebrations that followed.

It is also probable that Lehi would have used the time profitably by planting crops. This seems to be indicated by Nephi's statement when the colony was about to leave the Valley of Lemuel: "We did gather together whatsoever things we should carry into the wilderness, and all the *remainder of our provisions which the Lord had given unto us; and we did take seed of every kind.*" (1 Nephi 16:11; italics added.) Yes, we think several years could easily have been consumed in these activities. Moreover, the Valley of Lemuel camp must have been a safe place for Lehi to rest until the Lord gave further directions. Lehi had traveled three days beyond the shipyard town of Aqaba into the foreign nation of Midian and was, therefore, presumably beyond the reach of anyone at Jerusalem who still sought his life.

After the period at the first camp, the two families, now united by at least four marriages (Zoram was married to one of the daughters of Ishmael), packed up and moved south-southeast along the shore of the Red Sea to a place four days' journey away that they called Shazer. We scrutinized the map and estimated that in four days they could have covered about 100 miles, which would have brought them to the oasis of Azlan in the Wadi Azlan, which represents the natural place for them to have stopped for a time.

Possibly another harvest season elapsed before the families moved on in the same direction to Nahom, located at or near nineteenth parallel. Here the stay may have been lengthy, since the oldest member of the colony, Ishmael, died. (1 Nephi 16:34.) Surely, for his comfort, they would have tried not to travel; then there must have been a season of mourning before they pulled up stakes and moved on. Nephi specifically says in the case of the sojourn at Nahom that Lehi "tarried for the space of a time." (1 Nephi 16:33.)

When the group left Nahom, they turned "nearly eastward" and moved on until at last they arrived at Bountiful on the shores of Irreantum. (1 Nephi 17:1-5.) They had spent eight years in the wilderness (17:4), and would spend an undisclosed period in Bountiful. We tried to estimate how long it would take to smelt ore, make tools, build a ship, and grow seeds for their voyage. Could it have been as much as two or three more years? Allowing for a four-year difference between established Bible chronology, Jerusalem would have been destroyed while they were in Bountiful. Interestingly, by the time they arrived in America, Lehi had received a vision that confirmed the destruction of Jerusalem. (2 Nephi 1:4; see also 2 Kings 25:2.)

The Passenger List

We know that Lehi took his wife, Sariah, and four sons as he left Jerusalem. The party may have included daughters as well, since Nephi casually mentions "my sisters" many years later when they were in the promised land (2 Nephi 5:6); but they could have been born in the wilderness. Later the group was joined by Ishmael and his wife, at least two married sons and their families (1 Nephi 7:6), five unmarried daughters, and Zoram, Laban's former bondsman. It seems safe to estimate, then, that Lehi's party faced the desert with at least twenty people.

Why did Lehi select Ishmael's family and not another? It was convenient that Ishmael had five daughters, just the number necessary to provide wives for Lehi's four sons and Zoram. But was that the only reason Lehi chose that particular family? A statement by Elder Erastus Snow in 1882 may shed some light on the subject. He said that according to the Prophet Joseph Smith, Ishmael's "sons married into Lehi's family."[2] The Book of Mormon mentions "the two sons of Ishmael and their families" (1 Nephi 7:6), which indicates that Ishmael had two sons who were both already married when they left Jerusalem. Joining these facts with the purported statement of Joseph Smith, one can conclude that Lehi had two older daughters and that the two families were joined by marriage before they left Jerusalem. It is only natural that Lehi would send for the rest of his family so they too could escape the destruction of Jerusalem.

Simply for the purpose of seeing this band of travelers in more human terms, we speculated on the ages of some of the

---

[2]*Journal of Discourses,* 23:184.

When the group left Nahom, they turned "nearly eastward" and moved on until at last they arrived at Bountiful on the shores of Irreantum. They had spent eight years in the wilderness, and would spend an undisclosed period in Bountiful. We tried to estimate how long it would take to smelt ore, make tools, build a ship, and grow seeds for their voyage. Could it have been as much as two or three more years? Allowing for a four-year difference between established Bible chronology, Jerusalem would have been destroyed while they were in Bountiful. Interestingly, by the time they arrived in America, Lehi had received a vision that confirmed the destruction of Jerusalem.

individuals. We estimate Nephi was a teenager when he left Jerusalem. By the time he returned to obtain Laban's brass plates, however, he had grown enough physically that he described himself as "being exceeding young, nevertheless . . . large in stature." (1 Nephi 2:16; see also 4:31.) He had the physical strength to seize and hold Zoram (1 Nephi 4:31) and to cut off the head of Laban (1 Nephi 4:18). He was also old enough to have had great spiritual experiences, including a vision of the Savior. (1 Nephi 11.) Sometime later, he and his brothers returned to Jerusalem again and brought Ishmael and his family to Lehi: Nephi was now old enough to marry (1 Nephi 16:7), and his wife bore him children in the wilderness (1 Nephi 18:19). These considerations lead us to estimate Nephi's age when he left Jerusalem at about sixteen years; perhaps seventeen when the Lord visited him; perhaps eighteen when he beheaded Laban and seized Zoram; and perhaps nineteen when he married.

A similar review of the text led President George Q. Cannon to conclude that "Nephi was probably not more than fifteen years old" when he left Jerusalem.[3]

Assuming Nephi's older brothers were born at two-year intervals, we can estimate their ages. If Sariah was an estimated sixteen years old when she first gave birth, she would have been forty-four years old when she bore Joseph, her last born in the wilderness, not beyond the experience of many women then and now. By custom, Lehi probably would have been an estimated ten years older than his wife, according to our Middle Eastern friends—perhaps about fifty-four when Joseph was born.

Ishmael was probably older—as much as ten years—than Lehi. He had two married sons with families when he left Jerusalem (Lehi had none). So, if our assumption is correct that Ishmael's eldest sons married Lehi's eldest daughters, that alone would make Ishmael about ten years older.

The Means and the Way

With only six persons listed in Lehi's original party, how many donkeys would they need when they left Jerusalem? We estimate from nine to twelve to carry the provisions, personal belongings, and tents. We were assured by the Bedouins with whom we visited that each tent would weigh about 500 pounds and would have been packed separately as walls, partitions, and roof on three different donkeys. Thus, with three donkeys

---

[3]George Q. Cannon, *The Life of Nephi, the Son of Lehi* (Salt Lake City: The Contributor Co., 1888), p. 14.

needed for one tent, and a donkey per person for provisions, we arrive at a minimum figure of nine donkeys. The arrival of Ishmael's group would swell the number of livestock, of course.

After Lehi left Jerusalem, he could not have gone very far in a southerly or easterly direction before coming to the desert. As we looked at the contrasting terrain—steep, jagged, and rocky around Jerusalem, yet barren, sandy, and relatively smooth in the desert—we became convinced that Lehi must have acquired camels before he had gone too far into the desert, and probably as soon as he approached it. No matter which route he might have used to leave Jerusalem, he would have run into camel markets where he could have traded his donkeys for camels. He might even have had money with him that he used—leaving his gold and silver behind does not mean that he departed penniless. Those camel markets are still there, large, dusty, and noisy with haggling buyers and sellers.

We knew from fifteen prior trips to the Holy Land that there are only two ways Lehi could have left the city of Jerusalem. The eastern way divides into two of the three main routes from Jerusalem to Aqaba. We explored all three routes, but we did not follow in its entirety the variant route, which is still only a footpath over the steep Salt Mountain. Sa'adi Fatafitah, a friend who accompanied us over much of the route, had himself made this crossing on foot and assured us that it was still passable, though difficult. After examining and appraising all the routes, we found ourselves favoring the central route, which goes nearly to Jericho and turns south past bleak Qumran, west of the Dead Sea, although a good case can also be made for Lehi's use of the King's Highway. A person following the Qumran route east from Jerusalem gets out of town quickly. The logic of the downhill terrain helps explain why Christians at the time of Titus chose it as their escape route.

The west side of the Dead Sea, which at 1,290 feet below sea level is the lowest spot on the face of the earth, is not an inviting place. We saw utter desolation there; the mineral-saturated water lies stagnant in a long geologic fault. But we were astonished to find many freshwater springs along the western shore. There is also an excellent beach, which was regularly used as a trail in ancient days, according to Salim Saad, who had spent most of his life in the area.

It seemed to us that Lehi could well have chosen the west shore of the Dead Sea over the east because there he would still be in his native country, Judah, rather than the foreign nations of Amon, Moab, and Edom through which the King's Highway passed. On the west shore he also would have avoided the

Following page: The Wadi al 'Araba runs between Aqaba and the Dead Sea. During a rainy period, the *wadi* is filled with water; when it is dry, it becomes a trail through the desert area.

Jewish population centers of Hebron and Beersheba, where he might be more easily recognized as one whose life had been threatened while living in Jerusalem.

Wadi al 'Araba

We wondered about the geographical determinism that seemed to dictate that all roads lead to Aqaba. It was certainly easier for us to understand it once we entered the Wadi al 'Araba, the geological extension of the low-lying valley in which are found the Sea of Galilee, the Jordan River, and the Dead Sea. It is part of the remarkable "rift valley" system (along a geological fault), extending all the way from the Beka Valley in Lebanon to far below the Gulf of Aqaba on the Red Sea in the south.

The northern portion of the Wadi al 'Araba drains north into the Dead Sea. The southern end of the wadi flows south into the Red Sea. As we looked at it, we saw a wide, dusty sand plain, hot in the summer and chilly in the winter. High mountains jut up on both sides, from three to twelve miles away. Rainfall is slight, allowing the growth of only an occasional clump of grass or tamarisk tree. Other than the King's Highway, this plain is the only way south from Jerusalem. It has been intermittently populated by nomadic Bedouins from early ages. We saw many Bedouin tents, and goats, sheep, and camels browsing in the wadi; irresistibly, images of the ancient past passed before our eyes.

As our car passed over the beautiful modern highway, paralleling the ancient trail that is still occasionally visible, we tried to visualize the scene. With his whole family along and his animals laden with provisions, Lehi would have been no match for pursuers if there were any; and desert dwellers, expert trackers, could have been hired to track him down had he tried to hide.

A modern British explorer, Wilfred Thesiger, writing of his experiences on the Arabian peninsula after World War II, related an unnerving story about the tracking ability of desert Bedouins:

"A few days later, we passed some tracks. I was not even certain that they were made by camels as they were blurred by the wind. Sultan turned to a grey-bearded man who was noted as a tracker and asked him whose tracks these were. The man turned aside and followed them for a short distance and then looked at the tracks where they crossed some hard ground, broke some camel droppings between his fingers and rode back to join us. He was again asked, 'Who are they?' The man answered, 'They were Awamir. There are six of them. They have raided Junuba on the southern coast and have taken three of their camels. They have come here from Sahma and watered at Mughshin. They passed here ten days ago.'

"We had seen no Arabs for seventeen days and saw none for a further twenty-seven. On our return we met some of the Bedu and when we exchanged our news they told us that six Awamir had raided the Januba, killing three of them and taking three of their camels. The only thing that we did not already know was that they had killed anyone."[4]

However, we learned from our friends of the ancient and unshakable rule of the Arabian peninsula that may have been put to good use by Lehi—that of asylum. Once a sheikh agrees to accept a refugee, the tribe must protect him against any of his enemies. Of course, if the sheikh refuses him, he may be killed on the spot. Lehi, possibly acquainted with the desert sheikhs, may have benefited from this ancient code as he traveled from one tribe's jurisdiction to another.

Provisions

We know that Lehi took provisions on his journey (1 Nephi 2:4), and we tried to reconstruct what they might have been. We know that they included his tents, and probably such food as wheat, flour, barley, dried sour milk, olive or sesame oil, olives, dates, a few cooking utensils, bedding, and weapons such as bows, arrows, and knives. According to our research, no spoons or forks were used in Lehi's day among the Hebrews or the Arabs.

We had visited Bedouin camps on previous trips to the Middle East, and thus we warmly accepted the invitation of a young Bedouin boy we picked up on the highway near Beersheba. His family was moderately well-to-do by nomadic standards, but very limited in possessions by ours. As we approached the tent we could see everything they owned. There was a donkey in the dooryard, a horse and camel in the distance, sheep and a turkey walking underfoot. Entering the flap of the stiff black tent we saw handwoven baskets hanging on the center poles filled with cooking pots, some half-filled with waterskins. There were rugs and pillows surrounding the fire pit, with saddles and bridles in the corner. We could see their entire wardrobe in an old corrugated cardboard box pushed into the other corner. There were no windows, the only light coming in at the tent door and from the live coals in the fire. We saw no toys; in fact, Hope remembers that one little girl

---

[4]Wilfred Thesiger, *Arabian Sands* (London: Longman and Green, 1959), p. 55.

We learned from our friends of the ancient and unshakable rule of the Arabian peninsula that may have been put to good use by Lehi—that of asylum. Once a sheikh agrees to accept a refugee, the tribe must protect him against any of his enemies. Of course, if the sheikh refuses him, he may be killed on the spot. Lehi, possibly acquainted with the desert sheikhs, may have benefited from this ancient code as he traveled from one tribe's jurisdiction to another.

Close to the land Bountiful we found in the market at Nizwa, Oman, wheat, barley, asfar, sugar, pepper, and other condiments. Foodstuffs such as these might have been the type of stores collected by Lehi's party as they prepared for their journey to the promised land.

shrank back in fright from a proffered stuffed animal. The heavy, black, goat hair tent, with some white sections made from sheep wool, was anchored by ropes and tent stakes. The only water was in the waterskins. Graciously, they offered us drinks in cups rinsed by swishing them out with tea from their ever-present pot on the fire.

There was a women's section in the tent, and the women of our group were invited to try on some of their clothes and jewelry. The women all wear black dresses embroidered with multicolored flower and animal designs. Their heads are always covered with a shawl, which varies in color according to tribal custom. Black veils cover their faces when they leave the security of the tent. The men's clothing is simple, a long white shirt and sash (an Arabic word) in warm weather. In winter they add a dark-colored *aba,* or overcoat, made of coarse, handspun wool from sheep. It is very warm and sheds the dew and occasional rains. It also takes the place of a blanket. When our friends explained this to us, we understood why Moses had commanded the children of Israel, when they took raiment as a pledge for a loan, not to "sleep with his pledge: . . . thou shalt deliver him the pledge again when the sun goeth down, that he may sleep in his own raiment, and bless thee." (Deuteronomy 24:12-13.)

Since the living conditions of the Bedouin have changed little since 600 B.C., the possessions of the family we visited may be similar to what Lehi's group took with them on their journey. It is also quite likely that Lehi, despite his wealth, would have been traveling light and without any luxurious show as protection against marauding desert tribes that would naturally investigate a small caravan displaying many goods.

We were intrigued to discover that the one-piece Bedouin garment we saw in 1976 was clearly recognizable, essentially unchanged, in stone reliefs from Ninevah, now on display in the Israel Museum in Jerusalem. Sennacherib had this relief carved to celebrate his conquest of Lachish, a city of Judah twenty-five miles from Jerusalem, in approximately 701 B.C., only a century before Lehi's flight into the desert. The captured men not only wore that distinctive one-piece garment, but could also be identified as Semites by their distinctive facial appearance, hair styles, and beard styles. These were Lehi's neighbors, both geographically and historically, and we wondered how much Lehi's own dress and appearance resembled theirs.

Lehi probably carried his provisions in goatskin bags, which we found are still used all along the trail in the Arabian peninsula. Our friends corroborate our reading that goatskin bags, typically holding about four gallons, were indeed the standard method of transporting water and provisions. In a market at Aqaba, we found a waterbag of venerable appearance made from the skin of a mature, large-sized goat. The front legs had been sewn together with a rawhide. With the back legs tied off, the skin became watertight. The animal's neck was the opening of the waterbag.

This waterskin certainly looked old and well used, but we were still surprised when the man from whom we bought it informed us that it was at least ten generations old. Skeptical, we asked how a skin could be tanned so that it would be pliable and watertight for that long. The merchant replied that his people fill a new hide or bag with honey and camel milk and bury it for six months. When the skin is taken out of the soil at the end of this time, the hair drops away and the skin is thoroughly tanned. Our Arabian friends corroborated that this is indeed one of the known methods of tanning and that it was not impossible for a well-tanned bag to last a family for two or three hundred years or longer. We tested our waterskin after we got home; it has two small punctures and a patch, but otherwise it is still watertight and as flexible as leather gardening gloves.

At another shop close to Yenbo about halfway down the peninsula, we found two small goatskins, one black with age. They were swollen with the weight of the contents, which the shopkeeper said was honey. We wanted proof, and he unfolded and untied one of the front legs and "milked" a drop of honey out on our fingers. It was chestnut colored, clear, and very sweet. The shopkeeper gave himself a treat by sticking the leg in his mouth and sucking out a mouthful of honey! We declined further purchase but were impressed with seeing an example of this ancient storage method in our day of plastic, cardboard, and glass.

A Bedouin acquaintance described some of the survival skills desert people use. If their water is brackish from salt or minerals, they make it palatable by mixing a little sour camel milk with the water. Doing this every day makes the water drinkable. The technique also improves well water that is stale from standing. They call this mixture of sour milk and water *shanin;* it makes it possible for Bedouins to live on water that might otherwise be undrinkable. We were also told that a little sour milk mixed with water in a sweating waterbag would soon seal the skin so that no more water would be lost through evaporation. No doubt Lehi either knew of these techniques of desert survival or soon learned them by observation.

Clothing of the Arabs is quite simple and well adapted to their living conditions. The men wear a distinctive one-piece garment that has essentially remained unchanged for centuries. To this they add a dark-colored *aba* (overcoat) of coarse handspun wool in the winter. It is very warm and sheds the dew or occasional rain. The women generally wear black dresses that are beautifully embroidered with multicolored flower and animal designs. Their heads are always covered with a shawl, and when they out of the tent, their faces are always covered with a veil.

*Aqaba and
the Red Sea*

Although the population of Aqaba, even in modern times, numbers fewer than 3,000 people, it is still the neck of the funnel southward. A look at the map will show that there is no way a traveler could go overland from Jerusalem to the east coast of the Red Sea without passing through Aqaba; there are certainly no modern roads that bypass it. Lehi may not have wanted his family to rest long in the city—and, in fact, they pushed on three days' journey into the wilderness—but they would at least have replenished their water supply and maybe even stayed overnight or longer. By this time they would have been traveling in the desert for ten days to two weeks, and the oasis, with its stately date palms and brightly flowering oleanders, would have been a welcome sight for man and beast alike. We saw at least two dozen sweet-water wells, some only seven feet deep.

Archaeologist Nelson Glueck, who, like Lehi, approached the Red Sea, wrote, "Suddenly, as the camels ambled along [going south through the Wadi al 'Araba], new life seemed to spring into the group of weary animals. They quickened their pace, lengthened their stride, and, before we realized what had happened, the ungainly beasts had broken into a run. Mounting a rise, we saw what the camels had smelled. Before us were the waters of the Gulf of Aqaba, the eastern branch of the Sinai-split Red Sea."[5] Perhaps Lehi's group had a similarly exciting moment.

The clean blue waters of this part of the Red Sea shimmer in the bright desert sunshine. We have been scuba diving here and have found that the underwater visibility is an astounding 130 feet. There are huge mounds of varicolored corals that fringe that beach for many miles, and the clear waters teem with thousands of beautifully colored tropical fish. This spot would be a delicious change for Lehi from his ten-day desert march from Jerusalem.

---

[5] Nelson Glueck, "On the Trail of King Solomon's Mines," *National Geographic Magazine,* February 1944, p. 233.

The Valley of Lemuel

efore our trip, we had read some sources that assumed Lehi had traveled "three days in the wilderness" (1 Nephi 2:6) from Jerusalem when he camped in a valley he named Lemuel. However, the preceding verse of that reference suggests that Nephi started counting the three days from the time the group arrived at the "borders near the shore of the Red Sea," which must have been Aqaba. But something puzzled us in the text: Nephi talks about coming down "by the borders *near* the shore of the Red Sea" and traveling "in the wilderness in the borders which are *nearer* the Red Sea." (1 Nephi 2:5; italics added.) What distinction was he making? Once we arrived on the site it became more clear what Nephi might have meant.

The western Arabian coastal plain is squeezed into the area lying between the Red Sea and the mountains on the Arabian peninsula. Its greatest width is forty-eight miles in the area close to Jiddah. Called Tihama by the local residents, the coastal plain is the ancient route of the frankincense trail and the most logical route for Lehi's party as well. We determined about how far Lehi might be able to travel in three days and made a sweep on the map that distance south of Aqaba to see if we might identify possible locales for the valley of Lemuel and the river Laman. Naturally, we examined every wadi system, shore, and mountain very closely. We could go straight south down the coast in the Tihama about eighteen miles to Wadi Umm Jurfayn, which comes down through the steep mountainside to an oasis on the Red Sea called al Humaydah. This oasis is, in one sense, the end of the Tihama or plain, since a little way south steep cliffs fall precipitously straight into the sea, obviously blocking the trail farther down the coastline. The geographically logical thing to do—indeed, the *only* thing to do—is to turn away from the Red Sea and go east up the hills through the mountain range in wide, sweeping bends. Storms have long ago filled in the rough places with a sand and gravel "roadbed" for all of the twenty-five miles to the top (elevation 3,135 feet). People without animals could have traveled through the mountains south by inching up the steep and rocky hillsides or by edging exhaustingly up and down the jagged summits, but obviously the wadi to the east is a convenient "superhighway"— as the heavily laden camels passing our car in majestic disdain testified.

At the summit the wadi branches. One branch leads on out to the desert in an easterly direction. Another wadi slopes many miles downhill to the south in leisurely sweeping curves all the way to the seashore. This wadi, El Afal, runs parallel to the east

"And my father dwelt in a tent"

shore of the Gulf of Aqaba, but as we traveled it the mountains between hid the coast from our view. We drove down this wadi, which we think represents the borders *near* the Red Sea, finally stopping at its only oasis, a village called Al Beda, Saudi Arabia. There we were suddenly confronted with a military policeman, who explained in emphatic tones that we were in a war area. Since we were very close to Sharm-al-Sheikh where Israeli and Arabian soldiers faced each other over the narrow straits of Tiran, we could understand the tense situation and quickly complied with his request to leave, taking with us the images of springs of water and a luxuriant growth of figs and date palms.

We then pieced these geographical clues together with the description that Nephi had given us. Of course, our reconstruction is tentative, one problem being that it doesn't seem exactly to follow Nephi's chronological sequence; but his meaning fits very well with what we discovered if he was merely describing the kinds of places traveled through, not their order: We believe the borders "nearer" the Red Sea are the eighteen miles between Aqaba and al Humaydah, where the trail and the beach are practically the same thing. Then the borders "near" would have been the route where Lehi turned east and then south through the fifty-eight miles in the Wadi Umm Jurfayn and Wadi El Afal to Al Beda. (If they then traveled on down to the seacoast, that would be "nearer" again and would fit Nephi's sequence exactly.)

When Nephi later, after they moved on past "Shazer," referred again to "keeping in the borders near the Red Sea" (1 Nephi 16:14), he was probably designating the area about halfway down the coastal plain where it widens near Jiddah, when they were once again traveling further from the coast itself. But to us, our discovery of what "near" and "nearer" meant confirmed an exciting possibility: that Al Beda could have been Lehi's camp in the Valley of Lemuel.

Valley and River

Father Lehi pitched his tent in a valley by a river of water that emptied into the Red Sea. (1 Nephi 2:8.) Nowadays, in all the Arabian peninsula there is not a single river of any significance that flows year round and reaches the sea. The annual rainfall in this area is between .4 and 6.0 inches. There is a little more in the mountains of Yemen on the southwest corner of the peninsula and in the Qara Mountains of Salalah, Dhofar, in Oman; but still they do not make running rivers. Hence, there are no real rivers that we can identify today as the river Laman. Nor do ancient records disclose one. Had there been one, people would have been living by it for generations. But this does not end the matter.

Old Testament Hebrew uses two words that in English are both translated as "river." One word, *nachalah,* means "winter torrent" but is translated as "river" when it describes the Wadi al 'Arish or the river Arnon.[1] In both cases, these rivers dry up in the summer. We have stood in the canyon of the Arnon and seen a trickle no bigger than a man's arm at the very bottom of the streambed. But thunderstorms characteristic of the winter season result in a true torrent. Our archaeologist guide and friend, Salim Saad, told us that wadis run for two or three days after a rainstorm, and that in the Arabian peninsula the rainy season is almost completely limited to January and February. When the water rushes off the bare hills into the sloping, wide-bottomed wadis, "it comes with much force," he said, gesturing to emphasize his point. "I have seen an immense bulldozer washed down like a box of matches."

The second Hebrew word, *Nahar,* means a perennially "running stream." The word is used in the Old Testament for the Euphrates River and the Nile, both of which are indeed ever-flowing. Thus, Hebrew takes account of variations in the meaining of "river" to which our language is deaf.

It is quite probable that after seeing a thunderstorm upon the watershed of Wadi El Afal, Lehi may have referred to a "winter torrent" or *nachalah* when he described the "river of water." It is also possible that the spring at Al Beda formed a stream that flowed south for twenty-one miles to empty into the Red Sea. What may have been a surplus of water at that time would now be absorbed by intensive cultivation in the oasis.

We were traveling through the wadi during the rainy season, but were disappointed that for over two days' time not even one raincloud had appeared on the horizon. We stopped the car to talk to a Bedouin youth walking along the road and offered him a lift to Al Beda. When we asked him about rain and what happened in the wadi, he burst into excited speech, describing the run-off as *moiya kebira,* or "big water," and added that sometimes the water raced through this wadi for three days after a storm. It seemed clear to us that Lehi could have used the "big water" as an object lesson for his son.

The Wadi El Afal and the Wadi Umm Jurfayn were not our private discoveries. They had formed a main part of the centuries-old frankincense trail to Aqaba from the south along

---

[1]James Strong, "Hebrew and Chaldee Dictionary," *The Exhaustive Concordance of the Bible* (Nashville: Abingdon Press, 1890), p. 77.

the Red Sea route; yet we saw few significant buildings or construction on the way. There were a few modern flood-control structures but no Bedouin tents in the main stream of these two wadis. At the extreme lower ends of most of the small laterals that funneled into the main wadi, however, we could see tents and flocks. There was plenty of fodder in the form of bunch grass and tamarisk trees in the bottoms of these wadis, their bounty being peacefully munched by donkeys, camels, sheep, and goats.

We were driving on a new asphalt road that, as nearly as our guides could determine, followed the old caravan route. That would make sense since centuries of camels would gravitate to the easiest gradients and the camel drivers would adjust the camels' wanderings to the shortest distance between two points. If our deductions were correct, we were actually passing over the route that Lehi had taken in Wadi El Afal. It was difficult for us to express our feelings. If Al Beda had indeed been the camp in the Valley of Lemuel, then this was the base from which Lehi's sons had twice returned to Jerusalem. This was the place where Lehi read and studied the brass plates and told his family their own genealogy. Here Lehi offered up several burnt offerings. Here he dreamed of the iron rod and the coming of the Messiah. Here Nephi had his own vision of Christ's mortal life and mission with his apostles, of the sailing of Christopher Columbus, of Nephi's own people among the great gentile nation in the promised land, and of the ultimate restoration of the church. Here Nephi explained the allegory of the tame and wild olive trees. Here the seasonal business of planting and harvesting crops probably took place (to provide the "provisions" and "seed of every kind" they took when they left the valley), and here was the great celebration of five desert weddings. And it was here that, to the colony's great astonishment, the Liahona appeared outside Lehi's tent to give counsel and lead them to their unknown destination.

There are many magnificent mountains near Al Beda into which Nephi could have been caught away for his comprehensive and detailed vision of the Savior's mission and of the major historical events till the end of time. (See 1 Nephi 11-14.) The highest neighboring mountain is twenty-one miles northeast of Al Beda; called Jobal Al Lawz, it reaches 8,514 feet above sea level.

Lehi named the river of water running in their sight after his eldest son, Laman. Nephi makes a point of recording that Lehi drew a moral from the river for his son when he "saw that the waters of the river emptied into the fountain of the Red

Left: The Wadi El Afal may be the Valley of Lemuel. It cuts in a north-south direction from high in the Saudi Arabian mountains down to the Red Sea. Through these meandering curves filled with sand and gravel, Nephi and his brothers probably made their journeys back to Jerusalem. Further down the *wadi,* high mountains are on either side. It could have been from them that Nephi was caught away by the Spirit.

Sea." (1 Nephi 2:9.) Perhaps this implies that Lehi could not tell at first from his campsite, but only later, that the waters emptied into the Red Sea. Al Beda is located twenty-one miles northeast from where the wadi empties into the Red Sea.

An examination of our maps and geography also suggested to us the meaning of the phrase "fountain of the Red Sea." A fountain is a headwater, a spring, a source; and it is clear that the Gulf of Aqaba, serving as the northeast extension of the Red Sea, could be called the fountain of that larger body of water. Dr. Nibley had earlier shown how in ancient times the Gulf of Aqaba, like its twin the Sea of Weeds or Rushes to the west, was known in Hebrew as a *yam*—a "source" or "fountain"—to distinguish it from a large sea or ocean.[2] Lehi describes the Valley of Lemuel as "firm and steadfast, and immovable." (1 Nephi 2:10.) The modern appearance of Wadi El Afal is indeed that, its sandy bottom firmly delineated by the surrounding solid mountains. And so our hearts rejoiced. We had located a strong candidate for the site of the Valley of Lemuel. We also felt a special spirit in the Wadi El Afal near the oasis of Al Beda in Saudi Arabia.

Tents

Next we tried to visualize the details of that campsite where, according to our time estimations, Lehi could have stayed as long as three years. The most distinctive feature about our mental reconstruction was the presence of tents. There may have been as many as nine after Ishmael's family joined the group and the marriages took place, one for each of the married families. If the tents we saw pitched throughout the Arabian peninsula were typical of those the inhabitants had used for centuries, we could get a pretty good idea of Lehi's tents. Actually, this is not an unfair assumption to make, for historians say that the *beit shaar* (house of hair) has not substantially changed with the passing of time.

The Old Testament describes tents as "black" (Song of Solomon 1:5), made of "goats' hair" and containing partitions or curtains (Exodus 36:14), with a "hanging for the door of the tent" (Exodus 26:36). The houses of hair we visited and studied were oblong and had a long pitched roof with drooping ends. The smallest tents had nine poles, the three tallest down the center with three shorter ones running down each side. Guy ropes, also handwoven from goats' hair, extended outward to stakes (also called *nails* anciently) driven in the ground. (See

_____

[2]Hugh Nibley, *Lehi in the Desert and the World of the Jaredites* (Salt Lake City: Bookcraft, 1952), pp. 88-89. See Appendix I.

Judges 4:21.) Each tent was divided laterally into two or more living sections by a curtain or curtains: at least one section for the men and one for women and children.

We have no way of knowing if Lehi's tents befitted his economic status as a wealthy man or if he deliberately chose common black tents like the one we visited in Beersheba. We saw ancient but luxurious and beautiful tents in Cairo made of heavy, canvaslike material—probably wool or heavy cotton—on which careful artists had appliquéd flowers and geometric designs. The art of tent appliqué, according to Egypt's former deputy minister of state, Salah El Agamawi, has been handed down from generation to generation by women. The tent panels that we saw in Cairo were rectangular, hanging on square wooden frames that were set in the earth and lashed together overhead. These tents were like houses, with ceilings as high as twenty feet, and were richly furnished with rugs, carpets, mats, pillows, bolsters, and cushions. Of course, we also saw tents in Cairo furnished with modern tables and chairs, innocent anachronisms that testified to the utter adaptability of the tents.

These tents reminded us of a description we had read by Ibn Jubayr, a famous traveler in the twelfth century A.D., who gave us one of the best descriptions extant of the *Haj,* the Islamic pilgrimage to Mecca. He described one caravan encampment of an Amir of Iraq as "beautiful to look upon and superbly provided, with large handsome tents . . . and wonderful pavilions and awnings, for it was surrounded by a linen screen like a wall, in the form of a closed-in garden. . . . Within this were the pitched pavilions, all black on a white background and dappled and variegated as if they were flowers in a garden. . . . In these wall-like screens were tall doors, like those of lofty castles, through which one entered into vestibules and mazes."[3] Would well-to-do Lehi have lived in such luxury in the wilderness?

We were already familiar with how the more common Bedouin tents were constructed. Fifteen years earlier we had seen Bedouin women gather at Beersheba, bringing their annual accumulation of goat or camel hair. Together they wove panels for a new tent on an ancient loom that was owned by the entire tribe. They later presented the panels to a new bride in a custom much like our pioneer house-raisings.

A camel gives about ten pounds of hair a year; goats produce less. The hair is spun into strong threads by hand-held spindles. This thread makes a fabric as thick as carpet, very

---

[3]Paul Linde, "Caravans to Mecca," *Aramco World Magazine,* November-December 1974, p. 9.

The typical Arab tent, or *beit shaar* (house of hair) has not changed substantially with time. It provides cooling shade in summer and, with the sides down, warmth in winter. The tents are traditionally made of camel or goats hair that is spun and then woven into a fabric as thick as a carpet. Lehi's tents may have been like this, or they may have been more elaborate, with geometric panels like those we found on a tent in Cairo.

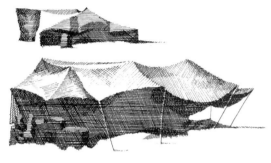

heavy and strong, but also very prickly and coarse. This is the "sack cloth" worn by mourners in biblical times (see, for example, Isaiah 32:11), and running a hand across it convinced us that wearing a shirt of it would have been true misery.

On this trip, we inquired more closely into tent-making; Naif Ibbrahim Sallam Abbu Mahfouz of Aqaba explained a less ceremonial and more continuous method of tent making that one family used. The accumulated goat or camel clippings of a year or two would be woven into a strip about one-half meter (two feet) wide to enlarge the old tent or replace a worn panel. The worn panel, of course, was never discarded. Even riddled with holes, it would serve as a side curtain. Thus, as new strips are added year after year, the tent passes from father to son, never completely new, nor yet completely old.

The "house of hair" provides cooling shade in the hot summer, yet with the side panels tied down, it is warm in the winter. Even though they are mobile, the tents are heavy, and it is obvious that Lehi would have needed pack animals to transport them. The average Bedouin tent is about thirty feet long and half as wide. A camel could carry one small tent; another animal would bear the tent poles, some as thick as a baseball bat in diameter, usually with one end dragging in the sand. The tents of sheikhs would correspond in size with their wealth, but they are built of the same material in the same way, in sections with lacings to fasten them together, each section designed as a load for a single animal.

Crops

Before we left home we had concluded that Lehi must have stayed several seasons in some locations to make his journey in the wilderness last an entire eight years. It would seem that one of these extended camping places may have been the Valley of Lemuel, where the group may have planted crops. The Bible tells us that Midian 800 years before supported an animal population of over 800,000 head. (See Numbers 31:32-34.) Consequently, it must have been more fertile than the eroded landscapes that we looked at as we drove through Midian. Lehi took provisions when he left Jerusalem, yet it is not likely that he took either a great amount or a wide variety. Nephi explains that after they had "dwelt in a tent" (1 Nephi 16:6) and had "tarried in the wilderness" in the Valley of Lemuel (1 Nephi 8:2), they "gathered together all manner of seeds of every kind, both of grain of every kind, and also of the seeds of fruit of every kind" (1 Nephi 8:1). Both wheat and barley were well known among Nephi's descendants (Mosiah 9:9), and rye was known before Lehi's day in Palestine (Isaiah 28:15). Perhaps these are the "grain of every kind" that Nephi refers to. The Book of Mormon talks of grapes, olives, and figs as fruits that its inhabitants knew. (1 Nephi 10:12; 3 Nephi 14:16.) Other fruits cultivated extensively in the Middle East in Lehi's day, even though they are not mentioned in the Book of Mormon account, were dates, coconuts, and pomegranates.[4]

It would seem likely that Lehi's colony either grew or purchased as many of these plants as possible while they lived in the Valley of Lemuel. Since they came from an agricultural area and since there was available at the campsite a "river of water" (which, even if intermittent, could irrigate some crops), they may have cultivated their own crops and probably enjoyed a relatively varied diet during this period.

Weddings

In addition to the daily agricultural chores, we know of five joyful celebrations that took place in this valley—five marriages. No event in Semitic life is more celebrated by a family or more anticipated by a daughter than her marriage. It is one day in her life when her importance overshadows that of a man. In the desert, preparations for marriages are very elaborate, since not only the trousseau but also a tent for the newlyweds must be made. Tradition demanded that the entire neighborhood population be invited to the festivities. To do less would not make a culturally acceptable marriage.

Lehi's four sons and Zoram, the former bondsman of Laban, were all to be married. Fortunately, there were exactly the right number of daughters in Ishmael's family. For Ishmael to have had five daughters old enough to be married was most unusual; many girls are betrothed while they are only children and are married at age thirteen. It was even more unusual that one of those daughters, the oldest one, was willing to marry a former bonded servant. Until she married, her four younger sisters had to wait their turn. It may be that no man had been willing to ask for her hand, and she could perhaps have been as old as twenty-five, a situation that could have been a great embarrassment to her father. All of these circumstances could indicate that she may have had some affliction, like Leah of old, and she may have considered it a great opportunity to be married, even to Zoram.

It was customary in ancient Israel for the father or kinsmen of a young man to choose his wife and arrange for the marriage.

---

[4]"Arabia: Vegetation," *Encyclopedia Britannica*, 1971, 2:169.

The Liahona was also called a compass, but it worked only according to the attention and faith the people gave it. It was given to Lehi and his family as much for spiritual guidance as for directing them through the wilderness.

No doubt Lehi, acting on behalf of his four sons, negotiated with Ishmael, even though the negotiations may have been mere formalities based on prior arrangements. Zoram, without family, was probably included in the negotiations as a son by virtue of Nephi's promise that he should "have place with us." (1 Nephi 4:34.)

If Israelite customs were followed, the negotiations produced five betrothals. Usually a betrothal began when the groom paid the *mohar* to the bride's father as a compensation for the loss of his daughter and ended with the wedding, a period that seldom covered more than a year's duration. During the betrothal period, the couple referred to each other as "husband" and "wife" and it was understood that betrothal included a covenant of faithfulness. The bride used this period to assemble her trousseau—and it would be interesting to know what arrangement those five daughters of Ishmael made, for their possessions were limited to what they had brought with them into the desert.

Marriage in Old Testament times required no state or religious sanction: it was a family affair consisting of a public covenant of faithfulness and acknowledgment of the marriage by the good wishes of family and friends. A fairly standard part of the wedding was a feast that sometimes lasted a week, enlivened with processions, music, and dancing. Considering the possibility that all five weddings were performed simultaneously, the celebration must have been lavish, perhaps including the local nomads as well in the festivities.[5]

Moving Southward with the Liahona
The camp in the Valley of Lemuel must have been a safe place for Lehi to rest. He had traveled three days beyond the frontier town of Aqaba into the foreign nation of Midian and was therefore presumably beyond the reach of those at Jerusalem who sought his life. But after he had accomplished all that was necessary at camp Lemuel, he was instructed by the Lord to move on, and the next morning he found a brass ball of "curious workmanship" at his tent door that contained two spindles that pointed the way they should go into the wilderness. (1 Nephi 16:10.) This "Liahona" was also called a "compass" in least five different places in the Book of Mormon (Alma 37:38, 43, 44; 2 Nephi 5:12; 1 Nephi 18:12), but it only worked according to the attention and the faith the people gave it (1 Nephi 16:28,) not

[5]See "Marriage," *The New Bible Dictionary*, pp. 788-89; and Madeleine S. Miller and J. Lane Miller, "Marriage," *Harper's Bible Dictionary*, 8th ed. (New York: Harper & Row, Publishers, 1973), pp. 421-22.

according to the magnetic lines of the earth. One of the points, from time to time, also had writing upon it. (See, for example, 1 Nephi 16:26-27, 29.)

While we were pouring over our maps in Salt Lake City, we had wondered why the Lord gave Lehi the Liahona at that point, when all his people had to do was travel down the well-marked frankincense trail. But simply because a centuries-old frankincense trail existed even in Lehi's time does not mean that Lehi knew how far he was to go on it, or where he might break from the more traveled part of the trail to pursue the lesser traveled portion. Thus, Lehi truly needed the Liahona. Of course, the Liahona was given to Lehi's family as much for spiritual guidance as for directional guidance in their travels. But looking at the scriptures and the landscape together gave us some ideas about its function as a physical "compass."

1. The Liahona pointed "the way whither [they] should go into the wilderness" (1 Nephi 16:10) as an indication to Lehi's party that they should keep going south-southeast rather than embarking on the sea at that point or going east into the mountains. This direction coincided with the relatively safe frankincense trail.

2. However, the trail was as wide as the coastal plain—up to forty-eight miles at its widest point. Caravans seeking camel fodder would, of course, use its entire width. A little farther down the coast, after Shazer, Nephi specifies that the Liahona directed them "in the most fertile parts of the wilderness" (1 Nephi 16:14), possibly patches of rain-fed grass as well as the more copious of the less-used waterholes.

3. The Liahona was the vital instrument when Nephi, with his newly fashioned wooden bow, asked where he should go to obtain food. The ball sent him "forth up into the top of the mountain" where, in fact, he did find game. (1 Nephi 16:30-31.)

4. Nephi does not mention the Liahona's directions when the group continued their trek, but surely it was the reason they traveled "nearly the same course as in the beginning." (1 Nephi 16:33.)

5. Further south and east, they had to make a decision about which route to take when the frankincense trail branches, one fork going south toward busy cities and the other fork going east on a more difficult route. Again, it was probably the Liahona that indicated that they should travel "eastward from that time forth." (1 Nephi 17:1.)

6. Alma taught his son Helaman that Lehi's party, because they were at times "slothful, and forgot to exercise their faith," "tarried in the wilderness, or did not travel a direct course, and

Right: We felt a special spirit near the oasis at Al Beda. The ancient ruins there are still called Jethro, for this reportedly was the home of Moses' father-in-law.

were afflicted with hunger and thirst, because of their transgressions." (Alma 37:41-42.) Perhaps some additional meanderings came from following the Liahona's directions to "the more fertile parts of the wilderness." (1 Nephi 16:16.)

An Ancient Place

An Arabian proverb recorded before the time of Muhammed by Lugman Bin Ad counsels, "Greet your campsite when you arrive and bid it goodbye when you leave, for every spot on the face of the earth has its own guardian angel." We had felt a special spirit in the Wadi El Afal near the oasis of Al Beda in Saudi Arabia. We felt the same tingle when we realized that this spot is also the biblical Midian, and ancient ruins at Al Beda are still called Jethro, signaling that this is also the traditional home of Moses' father-in-law. We reviewed the story of how this priest of Midian welcomed Moses after he rescued the venerable patriarch's seven daughters from harassment when they were trying to water their flocks, perhaps at this very spring at Al Beda. (See Exodus 2-3.) Moses became Jethro's son-in-law and a shepherd in the land, and followed the custom of taking the sheep far from the home base for pasturage as the Bedouins still do. On one such leisurely trip, he "led the flock to the backside of the desert [perhaps around the top of the Gulf of Aqaba into Sinai], and came to the mountain of God, even to Horeb" (Exodus 3:1), where he beheld the burning bush and was commissioned to free Israel from Egyptian bondage.

The Midianites, including Jethro, were descendants of Midian, son of Abraham by Keturah. (Genesis 25:1-6.) Thus Moses had married a distant cousin in taking Jethro's daughter Zipporah to wife. The Midianites, though nomads, possessed great wealth, for later in Moses' life when the men of Israel had been led astray by the Midianite women, he ordered the destruction of that people (Numbers 25:16-18); the army took as booty 675,000 sheep, 72,000 beeves, 61,000 asses, and gold, silver, brass, and iron. (See Numbers 31:22, 33-34.) Moses' experience in Midian was about 800 years before Lehi's estimated three-year sojourn in the Valley of Lemuel, but the parallels are absorbing and should make Al Beda doubly interesting to Latter-day Saints.

Shazer and the Place of the Broken Bow

Following the first directions given by the Liahona, Lehi gave instructions to break camp in the Valley of Lemuel. The group crossed the river Laman and then went in "nearly a south-southeast direction" for "the space of four days" to a place they named Shazer. (1 Nephi 16:13.) We calculated that this leg of their journey took them downstream to the shores of the Red Sea, where they continued down the Tihama. If we accept the seventy-two miles from Aqaba to Al Beda as the three-day journey into the wilderness (twenty-four miles per day), then a four-day journey would cover about ninety-six miles. This would bring the colony approximately to Wadi Al Azlan, long an important and large oasis on the Red Sea coastal plain, which may have been the locale of Shazer. The area is a stretch of sterile sand with gently rising mountains in the east and the Red Sea on the west. This route, of course, is the ancient coastal frankincense trail and thus would have presented no problems for city-bred travelers to follow.

Along this stretch of the plain there is no opportunity for a caravan to go inland, since the chain of wells lies down the Red Sea coast. Along the entire coast we saw water wells that had been laboriously dug by hand and walled with stones. In terms of the accessibility of the water, desert tradition regards water as the gift of God to man, not something to be possessed and hoarded, but something to enjoy, rejoice in, and share freely with others. Water is life in the desert; Lehi could not have traveled far without water for his family and animals.

If we are correct in assuming that the growing seasons of those eight years were spent in raising crops, Lehi must also have had to obtain access to irrigation water. We saw many ancient wells, springs, and cisterns on the route, flanked by modern drilled wells. The hard limestone well curbs on the old wells are usually deeply grooved where the ropes pulling up the skin buckets have rubbed their marks into the stone. Along the old trail in Saudi Arabia we saw primitive pulleys and scaffolds over some wells where donkeys had pulled to the top an endless succession of skin buckets overflowing with water. A wooden beam would tip the buckets upside-down where the water is channeled into a ditch. Then the donkey would back up, allowing the empty buckets to right themselves and go back to the bottom of the well to be refilled. But now gasoline engines pump the water up thirty or forty feet to the surface. Sometimes we saw continuously flowing springs with the stream carefully trenched to best distribute the precious water, but never once did we see a freshwater source without people and animals in the vicinity.

"And we did follow the directions of the ball"

Preceding page: Near the ancient harbor of Jiddah is a vast area of nothing but mudflats and sand. Lehi probably passed this way, for even in Lehi's time there was likely a village at the harbor. Perhaps this was one of the places where Nephi observed methods of building of ships.

On a previous trip we stopped by one well where a dignified Arab sheikh with beautiful Semitic features was watching two men digging a new well, and he explained that "we dig the well only that man and beast might drink." Asked how much he would charge drinkers to reimburse his expenses, he raised his eyebrows in surprise and replied, "Allah has requited me mercifully. In addition to these sons, I have other children and from God's bounty we have yearly an abundance in our tents. If I should pile up gold like yonder hill, what would it satisfy? Better we leave behind something by which our fellows are benefited." These are noble sentiments and come from a noble tradition that regards water as the gift of God to man, not something to be possessed and hoarded, but something to enjoy, rejoice in, and share freely.

Large-scale maps of the route that Lehi may have followed, drawn by the Saudi Arabian Ministry of Natural Resources, distinguish between dug wells that date back, in some cases, for thousands of years and the drilled wells that have been brought into production within the past few decades. If we assume that the water available now from the 118 old wells along the route is much the same as it was in Lehi's time, we discover that the average distance between each of these water sources is eighteen miles, the longest waterless stretch being sixty-six miles. The map shows us two sections from Aqaba to Salalah where water is so scarce that travel would be difficult. The first is the journey from Jiddah, Saudi Arabia, to Al Aunfudhah, which is close enough to the nineteenth parallel that it may have been Lehi's camp Nahom, where Ishmael died. Here water sources were spaced out an average of twenty-four miles apart. The second sandy stretch appears on the eastward leg of the journey, running from Najran in Saudi Arabia to Salalah in Oman, where water was found every twenty-six miles on the average. Interestingly enough, these two segments of the trip seem to have caused Lehi's party the most suffering, according to Nephi's account. (1 Nephi 16:20, 17:1.)

At various times we lingered by several waterholes to observe the parade of Bedouin life that our friends tell us has not changed within the memory of man. The men lead up camels or sheep to drink. While one man draws the water from the well and pours it into the trough, another allows only one or two animals at a time to come drink. It requires real effort to quench a camel's thirst after a dry spell. One camel can drink up to twenty-five gallons at a time. No doubt Lehi and his colony watered their animals in much the same way as these Bedouins we saw.

The Broken Bow

We were aware of the hardships on Lehi's party caused when water supplies were scarce, but as we traveled down the western coast of Arabia we also experienced firsthand the terrible heat and humidity that was another of the afflictions that no doubt befell them. Fortunately, our air-conditioned car sheltered us and speeded up the amount of time we had to spend in the seemingly endless monotony of the mud flats north of Jiddah. (One member of our group inquired rhetorically, "Can you blame Laman and Lemuel for bellyaching over this?")

In another place as we traveled near Jiddah, suddenly a violent sandstorm assaulted the car, rocking it from side to side. Blowing sand pelted the car body and windshield with a sound like hail. The storm lasted about fifteen minutes, with visibility at zero, so driving was out of the question. We huddled humbly in the car, grateful for its protection. Salim Saad told us that such dust storms are typical; they occur frequently and usually come up unexpectedly. Violet Dickson describes a sandstorm as looking like a brush fire. When Bedouins see that telltale sign, they rush to their tents and quickly take away the center poles, making the tents fall down on themselves and their families so that the storm can blow overhead without ripping the tents away from their moorings.[1]

But despite the dreadful weather while we were traveling through this area along the coast of the Red Sea, we were excited when it helped us realize how Nephi's steel bow might have broken and how the wooden bows of his brothers might have lost their springs. (For biblical references to steel bows see 2 Samuel 22:35; Psalm 18:34; Job 20:24.) The bow-breaking incident occurred after they had traveled "for the space of many days" (Nephi repeats that twice, both in 1 Nephi 16:15 and 16:17) and had pitched camp to rest for a season. This would have been natural for a party traveling at a speed dictated by the presence of women and children. Since Nephi says they again traveled "for the space of many days" (v. 33) to reach Nahom after leaving this camp of the broken bow, it may have been halfway between Shazer and Nahom. This would locate the incident roughly in the vicinity of Jiddah, Saudi Arabia, where the weather is a merciless combination of heat, humidity, sand, and salt—a force strong enough to destroy steel. We were stunned to see holes rusted through car fenders in a few months' time. Between March and November the heat

---

[1]William Tracy, "A Talk with Violet Dickson," *Aramco World Magazine,* November-December 1972, p. 17.

Nephi and his brothers depended on wild game for a large part of their food supply. Gazelles, ibex, wild asses, and other game are recorded to have abounded throughout the wilderness area that their party passed through.

is pitiless. Even in late January the temperature hovers around 85 degrees. Humidity averages about 60 percent year round, and in the more moist part of a fifteen-year cycle the humidity rises to a yearly average of 92 percent. Unpainted metal simply cannot survive such conditions. We saw little metal used in either local building or the shipyards.

Might this have also happened to Nephi's bow? Weakened by rust, it could have snapped in his hands when he drew it to its limits. The climate would also explain why his brothers' bows lost their springs at or around the same time. If they were wooden bows, they would have remained tensile and strong in the dry area around Jerusalem; but several years in the humid climate along the Red Sea's coastal plain, and even a short time in the vicinity of Jiddah, would inevitably have caused them to absorb moisture until they became as limber as saplings. In fact, acquaintances of ours often reported similar experiences with some of their wood possessions.

This, then, was the problem facing Nephi, but he records that he found wood to build a new bow. (1 Nephi 16:23.) Our archaeologist friend Salim Saad enthusiastically pointed out that the pomegranate tree, which grows around Jiddah, would make a good bow. These trees grow throughout the Middle East, even in brackish water. Pomegranate is a relatively straight and close-grained fruitwood that is remarkably limber and tough. Until a decade ago, Arab teachers kept a pomegranate rod handy for disciplinary purposes, and one friend told us that being struck once across the knuckles caused such severe pain that he reformed and became a model pupil. This made us wonder if, in addition to Nephi's possible use of pomegranate wood as a bow, he might have suffered from its other uses earlier when his brothers beat him "with a rod." (1 Nephi 3:28.)

Hunting

We do not know how long the family rested back at Shazer—possibly long enough to plant another crop (as they surely must have done in the valley of Lemuel) and wait for the harvest. Nephi's account (1 Nephi 16:14) suggests that when they again moved, still heading south-southeast, this time they seemed to have relied on hunting for their food. Had a crop failed? What kind of game could they have found? In any case, they kept moving until, "after . . . the space of many days," they pitched camp to rest and hunt food. Nephi does not mention a name for this campsite, but for the people it became Camp Tribulation, for Nephi's steel bow broke and the family faced starvation since the others' bows had "lost their springs." (1

Nephi 16:21.) Possibly the family again tried to grow crops while Nephi, under instruction from the Lord, made a new wooden bow and went hunting again.

The Book of Mormon tells us that Nephi and his brothers killed wild animals with bows, arrows, slings, and stones. (1 Nephi 16:23.) A local guide told us that he shot gazelles by the hundreds when he was a young man, just because he was "trigger happy." He reported that in the hills along the coast where Lehi's caravan had likely reached are wild asses, gazelles, oryx, ibex, reem (wild oxen), pigeons, grouse, partridge, wild cows, hares, and such domesticated animals as goats, horses, donkeys, camels, and dogs. Usually the dogs are swift greyhounds, trained to catch hare. Called *salukis,* they are popular among the nomads and almost every family has one. There are many other creatures that Lehi's party probably would not have considered eating but which formed part of the local fauna: wolves, jackals, owls, and snakes. Locusts, permissible under Jewish dietary customs (Leviticus 11:21-22), are also found in the area. Bedouins consider them a delicacy and dry them and store them to eat year round; even the dogs enjoy them. The locust season, which comes only once in several years, is a kind of minor thanksgiving time for the desert dwellers.[2]

Slings were another weapon Lehi's sons used for hunting, and our Bedouin friends showed us theirs. The men frequently wear them as ties around their waists, then whip them off, ready for action. Woven of black and white goat hair, sometimes dyed red, they are made with two long straps on either end, about as wide as one's finger, connected in the center by a woven pouch about three inches wide. They look something like a very large eyepatch. The hunter places a stone in the center pouch and holds the stone and pouch with his left hand and the two long ends with his right hand. Then he whirls the sling around his head several times with his right hand—until it reaches the desired momentum—and releases one of the ends. The stone flies out of the pouch toward the target. Several demonstrations convinced us that a desert dweller is accurate enough and fast enough to kill small game with such missiles.

Other Hebrews in Arabia
History and tradition tell of other Jewish and Israelite families that settled in this northwestern part of the Arabian peninsula, all the way from the time of Moses to the reign of King

[2]Ibid.

Lehi and his family were apparently only one of many Hebraic families living in the Hejaz. The great difference was that Lehi was being guided by the Lord to continue his journey, to build a ship, and to sail to a promised land. The others remained behind and were eventually absorbed into the surrounding Arab culture. This historical awareness deepened our appreciation of the close ties between all the children of Abraham. The Arab people are not only cousins to Israelites but are, in fact, brothers; and many of them are descendants of Jews converted to Islam.

Nebuchadnezzar. Sir Richard F. Burton, the famous nineteenth-century English explorer, reports a fascinating tradition of an Israelite army sent by Moses to purge Mecca and Medina (on the inland route paralleling this part of the western coast) of all their "infidel" inhabitants. They saved a young man of the royal family and some women and children. "When the army returned [to the children of Israel], they found that Moses had died during the expedition, and they were received with reproaches by the people for having violated his express command. The soldiers, unwilling to live . . . under this reproach, returned to Al-Hijaz and settled there."[3]

Numerous traditions account for the origins of other Jewish families in Arabia. One is that some came during the reign of David, with many more coming during the reign of King Hezekiah. It is well known in Islamic circles that much of the population in the Hejaz (a state in northwest Arabia) was Jewish when Muhammed rose to power in the seventh century A.D.[4] His first converts to Islam in Medina in A.D. 622 were former Jews who had written in their own traditions that "a prophet would preach in Medina in the last days." When they heard Muhammed's message, they accepted him as the promised prophet.

Thus Lehi and his family were apparently only one of many Hebraic families living in the Hejaz. The great difference was that Lehi was being guided by the Lord to continue his journey, to build a ship, and to sail to a promised land. The others remained behind and were eventually absorbed into the surrounding Arab culture. This historical awareness deepened our appreciation of the close ties between all the children of Abraham. The Arab people are not only cousins to Israelites but are, in fact, brothers; and many of them are descendants of Jews converted to Islam.

Brotherhood
and Faith

In Lehi's time, Jiddah would probably have been only a tiny village; today it is a city of a quarter million. However, Sheikh Shakeeb Al-awami, in whose beautiful home we visited, told us that as recently as twenty-five years ago a letter was actually delivered in Jiddah addressed only "to the man with two trees."

---

[3]*Personal Narrative of a Pilgrimage to Amadinah and Meccah* (New York: Dover Publications, 1964), 1:345.
[4]Cecil Roth and Geoffrey Wigoder, *The New Standard Jewish Encyclopedia* (Garden City, N.Y.: Doubleday, 1970), p. 136.

Now, of course, there are many trees. Water has been piped in from the mountains many miles away. The coastal plain, the Tihama, spreads out here to its greatest width. Through the haze we could see mountains in the far distance toward the east, but for the most part it is a perfectly flat and desolate plain. Today, there is a branch of about seventy-five members of The Church of Jesus Christ of Latter-day Saints in Jiddah, presided over by Las Vegas attorney DeVoe Heaton. He introduced us to some Arab business colleagues as "people from my tribe," explaining, of course, that we were not blood kin. That phrase made us appreciate the brotherhood of Christ's gospel, and we found it an excellent way to explain Latter-day Saint relationships.

In the teeming modern city of Jiddah, bulging with international businessmen drawn by economic opportunities in that oil rich kingdom, we also received one of the other special blessings of faith. As Lynn describes the experience: "My wife and daughter had come to Jiddah two days earlier and had trouble finding a hotel room, since women almost never travel unescorted in the Middle East. We had arranged to make contact at a certain prearranged hotel or through a mutual friend. The friends weren't there, and the phone number appeared to be a wrong number. Feeling near desperation I decided to go back to the hotel and ask the clerk to search again for a message. It was past midnight as I hurried back toward the hotel and turned onto a street I'd never noticed before. The thought crossed my mind that it might be a shortcut to the hotel, but suddenly something whispered to my soul, 'Check there for Hope and Cynthia.' I was in front of the Al-Rihab Hotel, one of a hundred in the city. Minutes later, we were united in tears of grateful rejoicing."

Shipbuilding
after the Manner
of Men

President Heaton took us to a shipyard at Jiddah, which was much like one we had visited up the coast at Yenbo. At both we saw men carving planks by hand, shaping the keel and bow with hand-operated drills in the same fashion as their fathers and grandfathers had done. There was no electrical power nor any modern tools. Such machinery as power saws, band saws, electrical drills, and pneumatic hammers were conspicuously absent; all we saw were hand-operated woodworking and ironworking tools, and they all looked handmade as well. We saw an adz, a sharpened iron blade used to hew lumber to

Arabian shipbuilders shaping and drilling timbers for handmade *dhows*. At Yenbo and Jiddah we saw ships built by the nailing method, while at Yemen and Oman we saw the sewing of planks lashed with hemp rope.

specific shapes. We observed local shipwrights using this tool to carve huge logs to the desired shapes for keels and ribs. We noted wooden and iron hammers and chisels used to skin off bark, clean up tree limbs, and notch the ends so the logs would fit perpendicular to the keel. We observed axes used to rough out basic shapes from tree trunks or limbs before the adz finished each job to the exact shape desired.

The hand-operated drill was the most interesting tool, and we were able to buy one at Jiddah. A hardwood spindle had been turned on a hand-powered lathe, and a hardwood cap, or handle, was carved to fit over the spindle so the spindle would rotate freely inside the handle. A wrought iron bit or point, which had been carefully hammered out with a blacksmith's forge and anvil, was fastened into the end of the spindle. This was rotated by a long rawhide thong held in a wooden bow similar to a heavy duty violin bow. The rawhide thong was wrapped around the spindle and the bow drawn back and forth to spin the drill, a process much like one the American Indians used to make fires. Although the process looked primitive and awkward to us, in a few seconds the Arab shipbuilder drilled three holes in the ship planks he was working to illustrate the technique and speed of his drill. He assured us he could easily plug up the holes with hand-carved dowels dipped in glue, inserted in the holes, and cut off flush with the surface.

In Yenbo we had been equally fascinated by the ancient-style saws used in that shipyard. The iron blade was stretched taut in a wooden frame, tightened by twisting a stick through a rope that connected the ends of the frame opposite the blade. Again, despite its seeming primitiveness, it swished through thick planks with impressive ease.

Wooden planes made of a block of hardwood hollowed out to hold a hand-forged steel blade wedged tightly in place were common in both shipyards. One shipbuilder had what looked like a regular iron chisel, but ground off bluntly on the end. This was used to tamp oiled hemp or palm fibers into the cracks between the hull. A system of notched wooden beams and wedges was used for clamps. Wherever the builders needed to bend the planks to fit the curve of the ribs, this ancient technique was used.

All of these tools described plus others we saw (except the adz) were mentioned in the Old Testament long before Lehi's day and were possibly known by him before he left Jerusalem (ax, Deuteronomy 19:5 and 21:19; boring tool or awl, Exodus 21:6 and Deuteronomy 15:17; saw, Isaiah 10:15 and 1 Kings 7:9; plane, Isaiah 44:13; wedge, Isaiah 13:12; knives, Genesis

22:6-10; measuring line, 1 Kings 7:23; plummet, Amos 7:8; stylus, Isaiah 44:13; hammer, Psalm 74:6; chisel, Exodus 20:25).

One of the shipwrights explained that the techniques of building Arab *dhows* or oceangoing ships had been handed down from generation to generation in tribes that specialized in this trade. His tools also went from father to son and were rebuilt as required. They were truly works of art, adorned with paintings and carvings, especially on the figureheads and the transomed sterns.

From other sources we learn of shipbuilding in this area at least a thousand years before Lehi's time. Drawings and sculptures convince us the style, shape, and size of present Arab *dhows* are not unlike those of antiquity. Modern techniques and materials are slowly changing the shipbuilding industry in Arabia, but the fading traditions of hand craftsmanship are defended by skilled men who learned them from their fathers. We heard of the *boom,* a coasting vessel, the *sanbooq* (average 70 feet in length), used in the pearling fleets, and the *baghals,* which reach over 100 feet in length. We felt that these large handmade vessels demonstrated Nephi's account of building an oceangoing ship by hand to be quite reasonable, even though we remembered that in Nephi's explanation of his shipbuilding he said he "did not work the timbers after the manner which was learned by men." (1 Nephi 18:2.) Apparently the shipyards on the coast had at least given him enough lessons that he knew, in following the Lord's style of construction, that he was departing from "the manner of men."

We marveled at the shipbuilders' skill. When they shaped each rib of their ship, they carefully chose a tree limb that bent naturally to the curve they wished and outlined the exact shape, chipping away with a small hand ax or adz. They preserved the natural bend of the wood, using their feet and toes to hold it as they worked. As we gazed out at the Red Sea, we wished that Nephi had included a few more details in his account. We wondered, for instance, what kinds of ships he saw sailing the waters.

Historians adequately document the shipping industry and ports strategically located around the entire coastline of Arabia. One ancient writer made a journey down Arabia's western coast in a ship and left us a record, *The Periplus of the Erythraean Sea,* dated at A.D. 57, or about six hundred years after Lehi's voyage. Its anonymous Greek author records visiting the village of Muza on the southeast end of the Red Sea, and comments, "The whole place is crowded with Arab shipowners

Following page: In the harbor of Yenbo, ships are still built by traditional hand-crafting methods. We saw many such hand-built ships that were capable of long ocean voyages.

Camels in Arabia are the single-humped dromedary. At first appearance they seem strange, ill-tempered, and quarrelsome. They grunt and complain and will bit nearly anyone within reach, or spit their cuds. However, their owners speak of them affectionately, even tenderly. Calling a man a camel is a compliment.

and seafaring men, and is busy with the affairs of commerce."[5]

Fish and Bread

The ships led us to another question. We do not read in the Book of Mormon that, during the severe hunger and hardship the Lehi colony experienced while traveling down the seacoast beyond Shazer, they ever once turned to the Red Sea for fish. The Red Sea contains many mackerel, tuna, horgie, and sardines, so why didn't Nephi fish? Having been raised in Jerusalem, was he afraid of so much water.

Salim Saad, who lived along the seacoast, told us that he had seen Bedouins in the shallows of the Red Sea near Aqaba wading in with torches on moonless nights and spearing fish that swam up to investigate the light. He also reported that many of the Bedouins are expert with the hook and rod. So, why didn't Lehi's little colony draw on the resources of the sea when starvation threatened?

Along the way, we accumulated more information about food. Village-dwelling Arabs have developed breadmaking to a high art. They use a very hot oven and enough yeast that the top and bottom of the flat loaf separate during baking, leaving a fat, hollow loaf. They tear these loaves in half crosswise, leaving two hollow "pouches," which they fill with food—and anything goes in. Street vendors in Cairo will sell you these *falafels,* which are a whole meal in themselves: salads made of tomatoes, onions, and cucumbers in yogurt dressing, chunks of roasted lamb, a delicious bean dish called *fool,* and a paste of chickpeas and sesame seed oil called *tahini*—all in the same hunk of bread. And unlike hamburger buns, these loaves don't leak!

However, the Bedouins in the desert have a different way of making bread. From one of their goatskin bags they scoop out flour, dampen it with water, add a little salt, and mix it into a thick paste. They pat the dough into a disc about a half-inch thick and six or eight inches in diameter, then drop it on a flat bed of hot coals. Naturally, the dough sears immediately. They turn it over to sear the other side, then bury it in hot embers heaped over with sand. Later they uncover the cakes, brush off the sand and ashes, let the cakes cool for a few minutes, and use them like spoons to scoop up their evening meal—a paste of ground chickpeas, liquid goat-butter, or soup—out of a common pot. There is no precise way of knowing when the bread will be baked right, so it can either be hard or soggy.[6]

---

[5]*The Periplus,* p. 30.
[6]Thesiger, pp. 61-62.

Desert dwellers of antiquity apparently ate the same kind of food that modern Bedouins eat. In the Israel Museum we saw evidence of produce that was grown locally back to at least 1000 B.C., including barley, wheat, garlic bulbs, date seeds, lentils, olives, nuts, and acorns, all of which would have been common staples in Lehi's time. They are the staff of life now, and were in ancient times as well. Our Middle East historian friends constantly informed us that the life-style of the desert has basically changed little over the centuries.

The Precious Camel

While we are cataloging foodstuffs, we cannot overlook the camel. To the desert dweller, the camel is more than the "ship of the desert." It represents a way of life, a special gift from God, a source of food, clothing, shelter, transportation—an animal so important that over seven hundred Arabic names exist to describe it in its numerous varieties, breeds, conditions, and stages of growth. Camels have a life expectancy of forty to fifty years, and female camels will lactate as long as four years after giving birth. Bedouins can and do live for months and even years at a time with nothing but camel's milk and dates as the staples of their diet.

Camels in Arabia are not the two-humped Bactrian animal from Asia, but the single-humped dromedary. At first appearance they seem strange, ill-tempered, and quarrelsome. They grunt and complain and will bite nearly anyone within reach, or spit their cuds. However, their owners speak of them affectionately, even tenderly. Calling a man a camel is a compliment.

On a prior trip to the Middle East, we saw camels racing over the desert. Our observations confirmed those of the explorer Wilfred Thesiger, who described a group of camels that "swept forward across the undulating ground with raking, pounding strides, their necks stretched out low in front of them as they surged up to the crests, and swept down into the hollows. But there was nothing ungainly about these great beasts, which moved as gracefully as galloping horses."[7]

The milk of the camel is so precious a commodity that Bedouins allow the calf to suckle uninterruptedly for only about six weeks. Then they cover the mother's udder with a leather bag and allow the calf to nurse only once or twice a day. The calf is soon weaned.[8]

[7]Ibid., p. 214.
[8]Ibid., p. 231.

Desert dwellers of antiquity apparently ate the same kind of food that modern Bedouins eat. In the Israel Museum we saw evidence of produce that was grown locally back to at least 1000 B.C., including barley, wheat, garlic bulbs, date seeds, lentils, olives, nuts, and acorns, all of which would have been common staples in Lehi's time. They are the staff of life now, and were in ancient times as well. Our Middle East historian friends constantly informed us that the life-style of the desert has basically changed little over the centuries.

Further along our trail after it turned east, we heard Sheikh Helwan Habtar of Abha, Saudi Arabia, explain that it takes about four camels to support one adult on the desert; thus, if Lehi had tried to live exclusively from his camels' products, he must have required a large herd to supply his group of at least twenty people. However, it is unlikely that they followed this Bedouin practice completely, since they also hunted wild animals and probably cultivated crops at various stopping points.

It is also likely that another harvest season elapsed before the families moved on beyond the place of the broken bow, in the same direction along the coast to a place that apparently already was called Nahom. Here the stay may have again been lengthy, for the oldest member of the colony, Ishmael, died. Surely, for his comfort, they would have tried not to travel during his illness; then there was probably a season of mourning before they pulled up stakes and moved on. Nephi specifically says in the case of the sojourn at Nahom that Lehi "tarried for the space of a time." (1 Nephi 16:33.) Two scholars have analyzed the interesting phrase "the space of a time" in terms of possible Hebrew equivalents and conclude that it meant at least two to three months, specifically the time for another growing season.[9]

---

[9]George Reynolds and Janne M. Sjodahl, *Commentary on the Book of Mormon* (Salt Lake City: Deseret News Press, 1955), 1:167.

Nahom and the Route of Much Affliction

Nephi reports that the Lehi colony continued southward near the Red Sea, eventually pitching their tents in a "place which was called Nahom." (1 Nephi 16:34.) When the colony moved again, "we did . . . take our journey in the wilderness . . . nearly eastward from that time forth." (1 Nephi 17:1.)

The modern village that is located on the Red Sea's coastal plain where the trail turns eastward is Al Kunfidah in Saudi Arabia. We had special interest in learning about Semitic funeral practices and burial customs, for it was here that Ishmael may have been buried.

The Bedouin women express their grief in a high-pitched wail, drumming their fingers back and forth on their lips. When a whole group of women are thus engaged in "keening," or *zaghreed,* as it is called, the peculiar sound can be heard for great distances. At the Archaeological Museum at Amman, Jordan, we saw examples of huge clay-pottery anthropoid coffins in which ancient Semites buried their dead. This custom, dating from the Iron Age, was practiced between 900 and 500 B.C. Each ceramic sarcophagus, big enough to contain a man's body, has a face, eyes, nose, mouth, beard, and long arms molded into the clay surface before it is fired, so that it looks much like an Egyptian wooden mummy case.

"...he did provide means for us in the wilderness"

Of course, we have no information on Ishmael's burial, but a photograph developed after our return shed interesting light on our suppositions. On the barren hills thirty miles outside Al Kunfidah, we took some photographs to show representative landscapes. Some ruins on one of the hills across from us provided a natural target for the camera. When we developed these particular slides and examined them under an enlarger, we found that they were not ruins, but rows of graves, their edges outlined with stones in Semite custom. We were about thirty miles from any village, in a desolate area. No doubt these graves were from more recent centuries, but their existence so far from civilization was another indication that rituals of burial were being maintained much as they had been many centuries earlier.

In the area of this possible site of Nahom, the shore of the Red Sea ends in one high, rugged mountain range after another, jutting up from the sea to a height of about 10,000 feet. The ancient frankincense trail leaves the seacoast at this point by splitting into a number of pathways up various wadis, one of which winds east from Al Kunfidah through Wadi Ababish over the crest of the mountains to the village of Suda. There this trail, which we followed, joins the other trails at the caravan city of

Abha, which is now a regional capital in Saudi Arabia some 6,000 feet high. It was inspiring to visit there and see the mountains drop away in a cascade of stones and wadis clear to the sea. We saw eagles and buzzards wheeling and soaring in the gusty winds that blew over this high mountain plateau. The weathered carvings and graffiti on the exposed rocks testified again that caravanners for hundreds of years had passed this way. Strings of surefooted donkeys were at that moment climbing the trail before our eyes, and the local Bedouins described for us the recurring sight of great camel caravans, loaded with bags of charcoal, coming up from the seacoast village of Jizan to the weekly market at Abha.

Our guide, Abdel Rahman, a forty-one-year-old Moslem farmer with three wives, took us over the old road in a lumbering truck past hills wooded with small scrub cedar trees. We could see that the mountainsides had been terraced to catch the sparse rainwater; more rain falls here throughout the year than anywhere else in Saudi Arabia, but there is still none to spare.

As we traveled up the mountainside, the time came at which all orthodox Moslems pray, a custom observed since the local Bedouins were converted to Islam thirteen centuries ago. Five times daily, the *muezzin* (caller) repeats each line and, lingering over the music of the words, cries out:

God is most great.
I testify that there is no god but God.
I testify that Muhammad is the Prophet of God.
Come to prayer!
Come to salvation!
Prayer is better than sleep.
God is most great.
There is no god but God.[1]

Our driver and his accompanying friend invited us to join them in prayer. We asked if it would be proper for us to repeat a Christian prayer and they willingly assented. As we stood in a line facing Mecca, they knelt down, touching their foreheads to the ground; then they arose and began again, repeating the chant a second and a third time. They were very sincere and solemn in their devotions. With all our heart, we petitioned the Lord for continued success in our quest and expressed our gratitude for the assistance we had received from such people as these. And at least part of their prayer we could join reverently. In great phrases that rolled like poetry, they prayed: "In the

Left: The Arab market in Abha was a surprise. Sombreros worn by the women were similar to those worn in Mexico, and we saw baskets whose form and geometric decoration could be American Indian. We couldn't help but wonder if these centuries-old crafts might not have been brought to the Western Hemisphere by Lehi and his family.

[1]Thesiger, p. 54.

name of God, the Compassionate, the Merciful. Praise be to god, Lord of the worlds!"[2]

A Town
on the Trail

At Abha, on the top of the range of mountains that Lehi must have crossed on his easterly route, we met Shag'er Ali, who volunteered to drive us out to show us old water wells. Accompanied by a friend who could translate, he took us into some remote areas of the countryside around Abha and showed us hand-dug wells, their stones chipped and mortared into place with primitive tools. Many of them still bear rope-worn marks from centuries of drawing each bucket up by hand, but all of them are now pumped by gasoline-driven engines. We looked in vain for wells where donkeys, oxen, or cows still pace solemnly backward and forward to bring up the buckets to spill into irrigation ditches, but in this area the twentieth century had supplanted animals with machines.

Also at Abha we met an extraordinary man—at precisely the time we needed him. Helwan Habtar, a graduate of American schools with masters' degrees in both political science and economics, took us to his home, where he recited for us his family genealogy back twenty-two generations. Intrigued, three other men who had come by for the evening also recited their genealogies back as far as thirteen generations. They were delighted we would make tape recordings of them.

We were fortunate to be in Abha on a Tuesday, market day for so many hundreds of years that Mr. Habtar could not tell us when the custom began. There is a market for honey, one for frankincense, others for myrrh, fruits, vegetables, cloth, clothing, donkeys, sheep, and camels.

Before sunrise the Bedouins came walking into town from all directions. The women were dressed in bright material, their heads covered with black shawls and their faces hidden behind gauzy black veils. This covering prevents "strange men" from seeing a woman's face after she is married, although the veil does not impede the woman's eyesight. We purchased a veil for Hope, and the Bedouin women laughed and nodded in approval. (All along the journey Hope had been noticed and thanked for her extra effort—apparently very unusual among western visitors there—to conform to Arab modesty by wearing black slacks under her dress, completely covering her legs in the fashion of the Bedouin women.)

---

[2]Ibid., p. 55.

Squatting on the ground Indian-fashion, each woman displayed her wares in front of her—gold and silver jewelry, vegetables, fruits, and fabrics. Our attention centered first on those selling frankincense and myrrh. Frankincense comes in golden lumps about as big as the end of the finger, while myrrh is reddish-brown and comes in rock-shaped chunks or as grated shavings. The frankincense was relatively inexpensive (a couple of dollars a pound), but myrrh is still costly because it is used for medicinal purposes: every newborn baby is given a taste of myrrh to warn him of life's bitterness, and burning myrrh in a censer near a child's sickbed is supposed to guarantee a quick recovery. A forty-five-year-old Arab in Jerusalem related how as a child his mother had made him jump over a dish of burning myrrh in Jack-be-nimble fashion when he was sick. Now we understood one possible reason why the wise men brought myrrh to the baby Jesus: it was to help Mary keep him well.

Arabs and
American Indians

The biggest surprise in the market was a group of women selling woven baskets and hemp hats that looked as if they had been imported from Mexico. The shape of the hats and the baskets colored with bright blue, red, and purple dyes made us wonder if American Indians had been to Abha. Our friend and guide, Sheikh Habtar, told us that when he was going to college in the United States, he drove through many of the western states and felt corresponding astonishment at the sombreros and baskets he saw in the Southwest, wondering if his Abha Bedouins had somehow been to America. The story of Lehi's group coming slowly through these areas and taking much with them to the promised land was, he said, the first logical explanation he had heard for the resemblances.

The small Bedouin tribe that make these colorful woven hemp baskets, according to Sheikh Habtar, live several miles west of Abha, almost directly on the 19th degree of north latitude. He commented that they had been coming to the Tuesday market in Abha (along the frankincense trail) at least as long as his family had been in the area, which was twenty-two generations. We have since compared the woven Bedouin rugs and blankets made on the east coast of the Arabian peninsula with American Indian weaving patterns and have been amazed at the similarities. Stacked triangles and geometric patterns dominate both art forms, as do the colors of red, blue, and black.

In his early work on *Lehi in the Desert,* Hugh Nibley pointed out that the nineteenth century adventurer Sir Richard Burton, one of the few who have known both Bedouins and Indians well, "was greatly impressed by their exact resemblance to each other." He added that one of his own friends, a Lebanese who had spent many years dealing with Arabian Bedouins and New Mexican Indians, claims "there is absolutely no difference between the two races so far as manners and customs are concerned."[3]

Traditional Merchants

One thing has changed greatly since Lehi's time: the barter system has given way to use of coined money, Saudi *ryals*. We bought a kilo of frankincense, a tangy gum that leaves a soapy taste in your mouth when you chew it, and some bitter myrrh. The piles of vegetables and goods reminded us of descriptions by the author of *The Periplus* and by Strabo, both of whom wrote within a century of Christ's birth. They told of the markets and merchants in seaport towns all the way down the coast.[4]

Strabo, who drew on the firsthand accounts of Aelius Gallus, prefect of Egypt, reports that "the camel merchants traveled [through this area] in the night, directing their course by the stars, and like mariners carried with them a supply of water,"[5] something Lehi may well have done in the same way. Gallus, who was sent by Augustus Caesar in 24 B.C. to capture the incense country, left Egypt with 10,000 soldiers, made ships on the west shore of the Red Sea, and crossed over to Leucê Comê, present-day Umm Lajj, where he intersected the frankincense trail. He was furious to discover he had wasted his labor in building ships when he could easily have gone around the head of the Red Sea and down the established trail. A supposed ally had treacherously told him "that there was no way for an army to go to Leucê Comê by land"; yet Gallus later learned that "camel-traders travel back and forth from Petra to this place [Leucê Comê] in safety and ease, and in such numbers of men and camels that they differ in no respect from an army."[6]

Gallus's army started their march southward along the seacoast. They had to carry water by camels, and the country began to take its toll, as hunger, disease, and fatigue decimated the army. Gallus captured Najran, the neighboring city east of Abha, and went into Yemen, where he besieged the capital. The lack of water and his army's increasing weakness persuaded him to lift the siege and retreat. It had taken them six months to

---

[3]Nibley, pp. 75-76.
[4]See *The Periplus*, pp. 22-54, and Strabo, *Geography*, 7:353-63.
[5]Strabo, 17:1, 45.
[6]Ibid., 7:357.

come down the peninsula. They were back at Leucê Comê in two months.

Strabo reports that the rocky shore of the Red Sea was completely desolate and that the local Arabs "are not very good warriors even on land, rather being hucksters and merchants, to say nothing of fighting by sea."[7] But Gallus built not less than "one hundred and thirty vessels of burden."[8]

Not many of the 10,000 men survived the long march, although only seven perished in actual combat. The majority died "from sickness and fatigue and hunger"[9] on the trail south of Leucê Comê, complicated by the treachery of their Nabatean "ally." This account helps us understand what conditions were like along Lehi's route some 600 years after his journey; it clearly suggests that parts of the frankincense trail were deadly to inexperienced travelers, and that the trail had enough traffic that some thought it could accommodate an army of 10,000.

The Route of Affliction

Lehi bypassed Yemen and the Hadramaut Valley to the south, which were then (and still are) comparatively densely populated regions. (The Minaeans, as nearly as we can determine, were the first to establish a kingdom there, in 1200 B.C. The Sabaeans who succeeded them were ruling in the days of Lehi.) In order for Lehi's group to continue eastward (as the Book of Mormon says they did) once they arrived at Najran, an ancient crossroads town east of Abha where the main trail turns south, they had to journey on a less-traveled, alternate route of the frankincense trail that skirts the southern edge of the great "Empty Quarter" desert. Probably they were following the directions given by the Liahona. Thus they avoided passing through the great pagan nation of Sheba to the south[10] with its prosperous capital city (anciently called Marib) and the agriculturally productive valley of the Hadramaut. Perhaps Lehi (or the Lord) did not want to further tempt some of the wayward members of the colony by exposing them to the temptations of the flourishing civilization that existed there. After having been in small settlements for years, would some members of the party have refused to go onward had they visited the major center to the south? On the lesser-used eastward route, in one place the waterholes are sixty-six miles apart. To us, this routing explains the terrible hardships Nephi mentions (1 Nephi 17:1) before they arrived at

[7]Ibid., 7:355.
[8]Ibid., 7:357.
[9]Ibid., 7:363.
[10]Van Beek, p. 41.

the tropical or semitropical area of Bountiful—and also helps explain his comment that through the discipline of these hardships, "they began to bear their journeyings without murmuring." (1 Nephi 17:2.)

Among those hardships, Nephi's mention of eating "raw meat" (1 Nephi 17:2) intrigued—and repelled—us, so we were surprised to find ourselves eating it in Cairo when our friend Angie Chukri served us this local delicacy. It was not dripping with blood as we had imagined, but was spicy with garlic and other flavorings. It had been allowed to dry in the sun until it was dark brown on the outside but pinkish-red on the inside and soft to chew, not tough like jerky. Though garlic was the dominant flavor, the meat left a sweet taste that changed our impression of the hardship of eating it raw. Later we saw raw meat for sale in Egyptian, Jordanian, and Saudi Arabian markets, formed in large loaves like bologna and spiced much like the pieces served us by Angie. Of special interest was the name the Arabs gave it—*basterna,* meaning literally "raw meat"—suggesting that Nephi's terminology was not merely descriptive, but was the proper term. Was this process, or something similar, the method the Lord showed Nephi to make their food "sweet" so that they would not need a fire in the perilous passage overland from the Red Sea coast to Bountiful?

The shorter but more difficult part of the frankincense trail that Lehi and his party took in turning eastward skirted the very fringe of the largest sand desert on earth. Stretching north and east of Najran, the Empty Quarter had never been crossed by western man until Bertram Thomas succeeded in 1928. A second explorer, Wilfred Thesiger, reported that he was the first European to travel between Dhofar in Oman and the north edge of the Hadramaut, a journey that took him a week. "We rode slowly westwards and watered at the deep wells of Sanau, Mughair, and Thamud," he recorded.[11] Perhaps Lehi and his group also drank from these old wells as they proceeded in the other direction across this most difficult part of their entire journey.

But even this more difficult and less-traveled portion of the frankincense trail was marked with desert graffiti like that found along the seacoast route from Petra to Al Kunfidah. Helwan Habtar drove us far into the desert east of Abha where he had explored as a boy and found petroglyphs and names carved into the rocks in undecipherable Thamudic, Nabatean, and even Greek.

---

[11]Thesiger, p. 71.

We flew, not drove, over part of this area. It was a rocky moonscape, barren and treeless except for an occasional bunch of grass or a small shrub. Broken rocks fissured by earthquakes and erosion covered the wadi-scarred landscape. We understood better than ever before Nephi's words, "We were exceedingly rejoiced when we came to the seashore." (1 Nephi 17:5.)

The Land Bountiful

Nephi rejoiced to arrive in Bountiful; we rejoiced to arrive in Salalah. All our research before we left the United States had led us to the conclusion that this little land, the one spot on the 1,400-mile southern coastline with enough moisture to grow any sizable kind of tree, was indeed the ancient Bountiful of Nephi's account.

We felt all the impact of that old story—never so alive as now—as we walked on the beach where Nephi may have explained Old Testament scriptures to his brothers, relating miracles that had brought the children of Israel out of Egypt; where Nephi may have testified of his faith in the miracles that the Lord would perform to lead them, as descendants of Moses' people, across the sea to the Promised land. (1 Nephi 17:23-32, 49-51.)

The old frankincense road comes through the desolate sand and gravel desert, over the Qara Mountains to the north, and down to the crescent-shaped coastal plain of Salalah, which is seven miles deep at its greatest width. The Qara Mountains encircle this little plain, their southern slopes covered with vegetation watered by the monsoons that only touch this place, and no other, on the entire southern coast of the Arabian peninsula.

Several wadis empty into the coastal plain. Ein Arzat, an ample spring, would have been a logical place for the two-to-three-year encampment that would have allowed the little colony time to prepare provisions and build a ship. Had Lehi chosen, he could have used spring water to irrigate crops; and, since Nephi specifically mentions "much fruits" and "seeds" among their provisions, they must have acquired them in Bountiful. (1 Nephi 18:6.)

We found that Nephi was not exaggerating when he called the land "Bountiful." It is truly fruitful. It springs to life at the touch of water, and the local farmers informed us that they make ten cuttings of alfalfa a year. We saw many fruits growing: citrons, limes, oranges, dates, bananas, grapes, apricots, coconuts, figs, and melons. We saw a profusion of wild flowers; white jasmine hung in garlands from the trees, and we smelled flowers on the breeze. Cattle grazed on the mountains. In well-irrigated spots, the grass was above our heads—over six feet tall.

Of course, if our conclusion that Salalah is Bountiful is correct, Lehi's colony was not alone there. This was the end of the frankincense trail, where the frankincense trees grew, so there would also have been farmers, merchants, inns, businesses, etc. In addition to the trail caravanners, there would

"Ye shall be led towards the promised land"

have been sailors and ships, for Salalah was also a port. It is believed that boats from both the west and the east sailed into this busy little haven.

North of the Qara Mountains, not on the more intensely rain-watered southern slopes, extend vast fields of frankincense trees. The actual coastal plain of Salalah has lush vegetation only where water comes from several wadis; otherwise it is as barren as most places in the American Southwest. But the southern slopes of the mountains (where the rain falls as the moist air rises) are covered with waist-high grass and clumps of great trees. Our rifle-toting guide told us that during the monsoon season the valleys are filled with mist and rain and the vegetation becomes luxuriantly tropical. Wild flowers and wild honeybees abound in the hills. We saw honeycombs stacked almost carelessly in hollow trees, and thought again of Nephi's description: "We called [the land] Bountiful, because of its much fruit and also wild honey [which] were prepared of the Lord that we might not perish. And we beheld the sea, which we called Irreantum, which, being interpreted, is many waters. And it came to pass that we did pitch our tents by the seashore. . . ." (1 Nephi 17:5-6.)

An interesting confirmation that the weather has not changed much in Dhofar over the last 2,000 years comes from the writer of *The Periplus,* who said: "The Frankincense Country is mountainous and forbidding, wrapped in thick clouds and fog, and yielding frankincense from the trees."[1] Other explorers who had preceded us found similar conditions: Bertram Thomas in the 1920s described the "thickly wooded wadis,"[2] and Wilfred Thesiger described "jungle trees . . . and on the downs great fig-trees [which] rise above the wind-rippled grass like oaks in an English park."[3]

We were puzzled by Thesiger's reference to fig trees, because fig trees are relatively small and have an extremely soft wood, not suitable at all for shipbuilding. As we walked the hills ourselves, we saw that they were not the usual fig trees, but were jumaise, or sycamore-figs, a hardwood that produces a sweet fruit. Some of the trees are so large that we could not encircle them with our arms, and most of them reach a height of fifty feet. The wood is very strong, resistant to seawater, and almost free from knots. Jumaise lumber is used for ships to this very day. Its ancient use was confirmed for us.

But if this place were to qualify as Bountiful, it would also

---

[1]*The Periplus,* p. 33.
[2]Bertram Thomas, *Arabia Felix* (New York: Charles Scribner's Sons, 1932), p. 100.
[3]Thesiger, p. 47.

need cliffs, from which Nephi's older brothers could have threatened to throw him "into the depths of the sea" (1 Nephi 17:48), an act one can hardly perform from a sandy beach. To the east, the shore curves away as far as one can see, but to the west, the Salalah beach terminates abruptly in magnificent cliffs that plummet about 100 feet straight into the sea. We climbed to the top by an easy route and there found fortifications for a gun emplacement. The view straight down to the churning waves edged us nervously back. Our minds were thundering with the question, Could Nephi have been threatened by his brothers on this spot, or one like it nearby?

Ore
for Tools

Our questions about the seeds, fruit, wild honey, cliffs, and trees suitable for shipbuilding were thus satisfied, but one major question remained unsettled: Where might Nephi have gone to find ore to make his tools? Conscious of our approaching deadline to leave Salalah, we had no time to ramble through the mountains, but local people told us of an iron mine in a neighboring province. Even if there had been nothing nearer in Nephi's time, he would have been able to make the ten-day journey to Jabal Al Akhdar to obtain ore there. However, we felt that Nephi had probably found his own source under the inspiration of the Lord, rather than going to a working mine, for he states that he made fire by striking two stones together and that he had to make his own bellows of skins to blow the fire. (1 Nephi 17:10-11.) Surely he would not have needed to improvise such basic equipment if the local people had an iron industry. We speculated on what he must have learned in the villages back along the seacoast and from the iron industry that was in full swing at Aqaba when he passed through years earlier. We could not question that ironworking was a skill known to Nephi's contemporaries. Isaiah (54:16) describes how the smith made steel from iron ore by using a charcoal fire. Adam's grandson, Tubal Cain, was the first metalworker, recorded at the very dawn of earth's history. (Genesis 4:22.) Six references in the Book of Mormon establish that the Nephites in America used iron and steel. (See 2 Nephi 5:15; Jarom 8; Mosiah 11:3, 8; Ether 7:9, 10:23.) No doubt Nephi passed these useful skills on to his children and grandchildren.

We knew from our research that an iron and steel manufacturing industry had been carried on since at least the ninth century B.C. at Aqaba (perhaps the first stop on Lehi's journey out of Jerusalem). So when we arrived there we were

Following page: It was into this sea that Nephi launched his boat for the long journey to the promised land. On the horizon may be the cliffs where Nephi's brothers threatened to throw him into the depths of the sea.

frustrated to find that King Solomon's ancient smelters are in a war zone. However, what we could see from a distance corresponded with Nelson Glueck's descriptions. Chemical analysis of the slag and ore taken from the old tailing piles he analyzed showed 59 percent iron and 10 percent copper.[4] These are very rich. Glueck pointed out that the huge mud-brick furnace faces into the ever-strong, prevailing northwest wind, a wind that has not changed in 3,000 years. These smelters are built of mud-dried bricks, with two neat rows of flues through which the wind blew, acting as a bellows.[5] Glueck says that the smelters were heated by charcoal, manufactured from trees in the hills near Aqaba.[6] This controlled draft of air, provided by natural means, must not have been available to Nephi later during his shipbuilding days in Bountiful, because he mentions that he made a skin bellows to "blow the fire" for smelting the ore. (1 Nephi 17:11.) The idea for this certainly was not his own invention, for his contemporary, Jeremiah, mentions the use of bellows in his writings. (Jeremiah 6:29.)

We were excited when we discovered a skin bellows in an old market area in Salalah, the very place Nephi may have used one. The bellows was hanging, blackened and neglected, on the wall of a blacksmith's shop. The blacksmith told us that such bellows had been used by his father, his father's father, and so on back twenty-four generations (an estimated six hundred years). We had never seen bellows like these before; they were not the pump type, like European bellows, but were more like an accordion. The neck of the tanned goatskin was tied around a wooden coupling tube that fit into an iron neck—which would, naturally, have been placed under the fire. This reminded us of a clay pipe, dated 1000 B.C., that we had seen in the Israel Museum in Jerusalem, a device that had also been used to carry air from a bellows to the forge. The four legs of the skin of this bellows of Salalah had been folded back and tied off carefully. The entire back end was open, with the skin fastened to two parallel sticks so that it looked similar to a woman's purse that snaps shut at the top. The blacksmith showed us how to grasp these two sticks in one hand, holding them open while we pulled the skin up, drawing in air, then closing them as he pushed the bag down, forcing the air out the neck. We were impressed that it really worked well, and we wondered how such bellows differed, if any, from Nephi's.

---

[4]Glueck, p. 237.
[5]Ibid., p. 238.
[6]Ibid., p. 237.

Seeing how painfully and how carefully tools must be fashioned in the desert made us realize the heroic stature of Nephi in being able to obtain ore, smelt his own metal and make tools, and then construct his own ship. His achievement brought to mind an old Hebrew legend dating three hundred years before Nephi's day:

"When the temple in Jerusalem was completed Solomon invited to a feast all the artificers who had been engaged in its construction. As the throne was unveiled, the guests were outraged to see that the seat of honor on the king's right, as yet unawarded, had been usurped by the ironworker. Whereupon the people in one voice cried out against him and the guards rushed forward to cut him down.

"The king silenced their protests and turning to the stonecutter, said: 'Who made the tools with which you carve?'

"'The ironworker,' was the reply.

"To the artificers of gold and silver, Solomon said: 'Who made your instruments?'

"'The ironworker,' they answered.

"To the carpenter, Solomon said, 'Who forged the tools with which you hewed the cedars of Lebanon?'

"'The ironworker,' was again the answer.

"Then Solomon turned to the ironworker: 'Thou art all men's father in art. Go, wash the sweat of the forge from thy face and sit at my right hand.'"[7]

When the Lord commanded Nephi to construct a ship after the manner that the Lord would show him, Nephi said: "Lord, whither shall I go that I may find ore to molten, that I may make tools to construct the ship after the manner which thou hast shown unto me?" (1 Nephi 17:9.) Apparently because he learned to be an ironworker, maybe even as a boy in Jerusalem or, more likely, because he learned en route at Aqaba or some other place (possibly even Salalah itself), Nephi had no need to ask the Lord *how* to work the ore to make tools but only *where* to get it.

Building the Ship
We indulged in trying to imagine the ship that Nephi might have built. Accustomed to industrial methods as we were, we had been surprised repeatedly by the traditions of craftsmanship we saw as we came down the coast, each generation inheriting the knowledge of the previous generations. In Yenbo, Saudi Arabia, we asked one shipbuilder where his plans

---

[7]Douglas Allen Fisher. *The Epic of Steel* (New York: Harper and Row, 1963), p. 5.

When Lehi and his party came into the land they called Bountiful, the sight of tall grass, trees, and flowers must have seemed heaven-sent. After wandering in the wilderness for years, they had come to the only place on the southern shore of the Arabian peninsula that receives enough rain and moisture to support dense vegetation. Several springs flow from the Qara mountains and water the fertile plain below. These large sycamore fig trees were photographed during the dry season; during the rainy season the area becomes luxuriant, and we saw many trees that had grown to well over 60 feet in height.

were; he pointed to his head.[8] In this man's mind were plans sufficiently detailed for him to lay out the dimensions of the ship he was building, to fasten ribs to keel, and to join planks to ribs without reference to any written diagram.

We noticed two basic patterns of shipbuilding in shipyards in Jiddah and Salalah. In each case, the builder laid the keel and fastened the ribs to the keel. The ribs were always made out of tree limbs whose curve provided the desired angle for the ribs. Planks were fastened to the skeleton either by nailing or by "sewing." In the first method, the builder drilled through the plank and rib with an iron-tipped hand drill. Through the hole, he drove a large iron spike with oiled hemp packing wrapped around the shaft under the large head. The spike was then bent over on the inside to cinch the nail in place.

In the sewing method, the builder drilled a series of holes wherever the planks were joined together; then he lashed them tightly together with hemp rope and waterproofed the lashings. The planks were sewn to the ribs in much the same way. We were intrigued that this method of shipbuilding was used only in Yemen and Oman and apparently dates far back in antiquity. The nailing method was used in Yenbo and Jiddah.

Steel ships have largely replaced the great wooden Arabian *dhows* that plied the seas in centuries past, but the ships still being built by hand are remarkably fine. They have carved figureheads, custom-designed transomsterns, and quarter galleries.[9]

In building his own ship, Nephi could have cut down trees and dragged them to the sandy beach using camel power, or he could have purchased dressed lumber from the local people. He does not tell us how he got his timbers, but he does comment that the completed ship "was good, and that the workmanship thereof was exceeding fine." (1 Nephi 18:4.)

As we have noted before, Nephi did not build the ship "after the manner of men," but "after the manner which the Lord had shown unto" him. (1 Nephi 18:2.) Our examination of ancient shipbuilding serves only to illustrate that for him to have been acquainted with contemporary construction techniques ("the manner of men") was not extraordinary or unlikely. He built in an area where shipbuilding was well-known. Indeed, even though his ship was not "after the manner of men," he may well have used a number of the methods and elements of design or building techniques that were known to the people of his time, the Lord directing him

[8]For an account of a similar incident, see Clifford Hawkins, "Ghost Ships in the Gulf," *Aramco World Magazine,* March-April 1974, 25:29.
[9]Ibid.

mainly in the unknown matters necessary to make a ship able to carry them on the extraordinary trip across the Pacific to South America.

An Ocean-going Vessel

We estimated that, with the birth of children, Lehi's colony may have numbered at least forty-nine people at the time of embarkation: seventeen adults and thirty-two children, estimating an average of four children from seven of the marriages in eight years, two more sons (Joseph and Jacob) born to Lehi and Sariah, and children that the two sons of Ishmael had prior to their departure from Jerusalem. (1 Nephi 7:6.) The families may have had more children than this, even as many as sixty-five or so. To accommodate a group of this size, we figured that a ship would have to be at least sixty feet long. (We saw several vessels of this size being built by hand and without written plans in the shipyards we visited.) In addition to the people, the ship would also need to carry enough fruit, meat, honey, provisions, seeds, tents, and personal items to supply the colony. (1 Nephi 18:6.) A sixty-foot-long ship would not have been excessively large; many of the *dhows* now sailing the Indian Ocean and the Red Sea are as large as 180 feet, all handmade. No doubt Nephi's ship had a wide deck, since we are informed that the brothers and their wives made merry on the ship with their singing and dancing. (1 Nephi 18:9.) Dancing would have been impossible if the ship had only ribs and planking. Nephi's ship also probably had sails and a rudder or some other way to steer it, because Nephi says he "did guide the ship." (1 Nephi 18:22.)

We asked a shipwright how many working days would be required to build a sixty-foot-long vessel. He estimated that the thirty-five men working in his shipyard could do it in forty-five days, or a total of 1,575 man days. At least part of the time, Nephi had the labor of eight men in his father's colony, and possibly some of the children. Working together, they could perhaps have built such a ship in approximately 200 working days. Of course, if the ship were bigger, and it could well have been, more time would have been needed. Nonworking days would include Sabbath days, Jewish festival days, and the days that Nephi worked alone before the others started to help him. It is thus easy to see that it could have taken at least ten to twelve months to build the ship. Assuming that all the men could not be working on the boat all of the time—because of sickness, family concerns, hunting, planting, harvesting, etc.—a more likely time span for building the ship would be well over a year.

In Salalah we confirmed the fact that the monsoons, which fill the Qara Mountains with life-giving moisture during the summer, also provide Salalah with a trade wind that could have taken the ship toward the Pacific. As shipping records indicate, the trade winds have, from ancient times, consistently come from the northeast during October through May; from June to September, the winds come from the southwest.

And since Nephi also had to smelt the iron, make the tools, and probably cut and dress his own lumber, the shipbuilding project could easily have taken about two years.

Truly it was a miracle for Nephi to construct a ship that would take so many people safely on such a long voyage. His nation had experimented with a navy during the time of Solomon, but Hiram of Tyre had provided the experienced seamen. (1 Kings 9:26-27.) Judges 5:17 alludes to a seagoing experience of the tribes of Dan and Asher, but the Phoenicians and Philistines held most of the seacoast, curtailing Hebrew experience there. When King Jehoshaphat of Judah attempted to revive the shipping industry at Aqaba, seventy years after Solomon, the ships were destroyed before they could even set sail. (2 Chronicles 20:35-36; 1 Kings 22:48-49.) The Hebrews were normally very limited in their understanding of the sea.

Favorable Winds

In Salalah we confirmed the fact that the monsoons, which fill the Qara Mountains with life-giving moisture during the summer, also provide Salalah with a trade wind that could have taken the ship toward the Pacific. As shipping records indicate, the trade winds have, from ancient times, consistently come from the northeast during October through May; from June to September, the winds come from the southwest.

Ships had existed for centuries before Lehi's time along the coast of southern Arabia, and it is indisputable that Arabians had explored for hundreds of miles along the coastline. But the first record we were able to find of anyone sailing on the open sea is from the first century A.D., when a Roman navigator, Hippalus, learned of the seasonal winds from the Arabs and opened a new trade route across the open sea between the Red Sea and India.[10] "It was a sensational discovery and soon the peoples of the area were voyaging down the Arabian coast, through the Straits of Hormuz, across the Indian Ocean, along the Hadhramaut, up into the Red Sea or down the coast of East Africa" on the strength of these winds.[11]

By the sixth century A.D., Arab entrepreneurs were sailing their *dhows* all the way from the Arabian peninsula to China. Arab ships rode the monsoons to the Malibar coast of India, then on to Ceylon in time to catch the summer monsoon (June to September) and speed across the often treacherous Bay of Bengal, past the Nicobar Islands, through the Malacca Straits,

---

[10]"Geography: Romans," *Encyclopedia Britannica*, 1971, *10:146*.
[11]Hawkins, p. 26. See also *Oman in Colour* (England: Ministry of Information and Tourism, Sultanate of Oman, 1974), p. iv.

and into the South China Sea. From here they were able to make a quick, if risky, thirty-day run up to the main trading station at Canton in China. The trip from the Arabian peninsula to China took approximately 120 days of straight sailing, or six months counting provisioning stops along the way.[12]

Once they emerged from the Malacca Straits, the *dhows* would sometimes be blown completely off course and would end up in the Pacific "where, the Chinese believed, the drain spout of the world's ocean sucked the unwary sailor into oblivion."[13]

All of these records date from at least five hundred years after Lehi's party left Arabia; but the existence of coastal shipping and the monsoons may have been the combination of events that enabled Nephi, inspired of the Lord, to push off into the deep, charting a course that may not have been followed again until five centuries had elapsed. And if it took later sailors 120 days to sail from Arabia to China, it would possibly have taken Nephi one year to fifteen months to cover the three-times-longer distance between Arabia and South America. That voyage is a great testament of faith and courage and an inspiring tribute to Nephi's ship. What a story remains to be told!

Conclusions

On the coast of Salalah, we believe that we found the end of Lehi's trail from Jerusalem to Bountiful. We discovered no contradictions, no absurdities in the record Nephi had left behind him. Nothing that we discovered in the volumes on geography and history contradicted that ancient prophet. On the contrary, corroboration of his account came from dozens of sources, showing that only someone who had passed through there in person and had experienced the rigors of the trip could have given the amazing details that, even 2,560 years later, seemed to harmonize with what we saw.

Although they are by nature tentative, here are a few of our conclusions.

1. The Arabian peninsula, through which Lehi's route in 600 B.C. went, was not an unpopulated wilderness, but a land where many people had worked out a precise and precarious relationship to their water-poor land.

2. Frankincense, produced in Salalah, Oman, on the Arabian Sea since at least 1500 B.C. (and *only* there until long after Lehi), was in such demand in the ancient world that huge

---

[12]Nancy Jenkins, "The China Trade," *Aramco World Magazine*, July-August 1975, 26:24, 26-27.
[13]Ibid., p. 27.

trade routes had been established. The constant travel of men, camels, news, and wealth kept the Arabian peninsula from being isolated from the rest of the Middle East.

3. Thousands of people made similar journeys to Salalah that Lehi probably made. Their experiences, recorded in ancient documents and in less obvious evidence of pictographs, hand-dug wells, and well-preserved traditions, confirm that the trip was not an easy one. The protection and guidance of the Lord was necessary to the success of Lehi's little colony.

4. We feel that we found reasonable evidence for suggesting Wadi El Afal in Saudi Arabia as the Valley of Lemuel, and even more conclusive evidence that Salalah in Oman is the land Bountiful.

5. The weather and geography there have changed little, if any, since Lehi's day.

6. Lehi quite likely adopted the life-style of the nomadic Arabian tribes for the years of his Arabian journey, including the custom of living in tents and the methods of finding water, food, and transporting people and provisions mainly by camel.

7. Some North and South American Indian art forms appear to have originated among the Semitic peoples of Arabia, or possibly both cultures derived their art forms from some common source.

8. Nephi could have been exposed to both ironmaking and shipbuilding while traveling southward.

9. There is much yet to be learned from the accumulated records and traditions of the Arabs that Latter-day Saints will find helpful.

Through our experience, we felt, as never before, the truthfulness of the Book of Mormon account. We felt the Lord's protection and guidance in our travels and look forward with faith and excitement to future discoveries that will testify to Joseph Smith's great work.

Appendix I   # The Writings of Hugh Nibley

The major Latter-day Saint source in our preparation to search for Lehi's trail, a kind of "locus classicus" of thinking in the Church about Lehi's cultural and geographical connection to the Arabian desert, was Dr. Hugh Nibley's series of articles titled "Lehi in the Desert," which appeared in the Improvement Era *in 1950. Following is the slightly changed version, from the book* Lehi in the Desert and the World of the Jaredites *(Salt Lake City: Bookcraft, 1952), pp. 124-28. This version includes reference to material on Lehi's trail by Frederick G. Williams, which Dr. Nibley (after his articles were first published) discovered in an article by Elder John A. Widtsoe, and which he felt substantiated his independently developed theory about the major elements of the route and its ending point in modern Oman.*

After traveling a vast distance in a south-southeasterly direction (1 Nephi 16:14, 33), the party struck off almost due eastward through the worst desert of all, where they "did wade through much affliction," to emerge in a state of almost complete exhaustion into a totally unexpected paradise by the sea. There is such a paradise in the Qara Mountains on the southern coast of Arabia. To reach it by moving "nearly eastward" (17:1) from the Red Sea coast, one would have to turn east on the nineteenth parallel. In *The Improvement Era* for September 1951 the present writer published a map in which his main concern was to make Lehi reach the sea in the forested sector of the Hadhramaut, and no other consideration dictated his sketching of the map. He foolishly overlooked the fact that Dr. John A. Widtsoe had published in the *Era* some months previously what purports to be, and probably is, a genuine "Revelation to Joseph the Seer," in which it is stated that Lehi's party "traveled nearly a south, southeast direction until they came to the nineteenth degree of north latitude; then nearly east to the sea of Arabia. . . ."[15] By an interesting coincidence, the route shown in the author's map turned east exactly at the nineteenth parallel. This correlation of data from two totally different sources is a strong indication that both are correct. The only other possible route would have been down the *western* shore of the Red Sea from Necho's canal, and on such a course one cannot turn eastward until passing the tenth parallel, and then it is not the Arabian Sea that one finds but the Indian Ocean. Along with this, certain other rigorous conditions must be fulfilled which can only be met on the south coast of Arabia.

Of the Qara Mountains which lie in that limited sector of the coast of south Arabia which Lehi *must* have reached if he turned east at the nineteenth parallel, Bertram Thomas, one of the few Europeans who has ever seen them, writes:

"What a glorious place! Mountains three thousand feet high basking above a tropical ocean, their seaward slopes velvety with waving jungle, their roofs, fragrant with rolling yellow meadows, beyond which the mountains slope north-wards to a red sandstone steppe. . . . Great was my delight when in 1928 I suddenly came upon it all from out of the arid wastes of the southern borderlands."

Captain Thomas (whom Lowell Thomas calls "the greatest living explorer") goes on to describe the aromatic shrubs of the place, the wooded valleys, "the hazy rim of the distant sea lifted beyond the mountains rolling down to it," and the wondrous beauty of the "sylvan scenes" that opened to the view as he passed down through the lush forests to the sea.[16]

Compare this with Nephi's picture,

"And we did come to the land which we called Bountiful, because of its much fruit and also wild honey. . . . And we beheld the sea . . . and notwithstanding we had suffered many afflictions and much difficulty, yea, even so much that we cannot write them all, we were exceedingly rejoiced when we came to the seashore; and we called the place Bountiful, because of its much fruit . . . And . . . the voice of the Lord came unto me, saying: Arise and get thee into the mountain. . . ." (I Ne. 17:5-7.)

It is virtually the same scene: the mountains, the rich woodlands with timber for ships, the rolling yellow meadow a paradise for bees, the view of the sea beyond, and above all the joyful relief at the sudden emergence from the "red sandstone steppe," one of the worst deserts on earth. Thomas, of course, was not interested in finding honey, but for those who must live permanently in the desert there is no greater treasure than a find of honey, as a great number of roots and derivative words in the Arabic vocabulary makes clear.[17] Much the same description might suit the mountains of Oman farther east and lying on the twenty-fifth parallel, the discovery of which came as a great surprise in 1838.[18] When in 1843 Von Wrede gave a glowing description of the mountains of the Hadramaut to which Lehi came, the great Von Humboldt and, following him, of course, the whole learned world, simply refused to believe him.[18] Thomas' delectable mountains were unknown to the west until less than twenty-five years ago. Though "the southern coasts of Arabia had admirable harbors," they appear not to have been used, with a few possible exceptions, until well after the time of Christ.[19]

Watching Lehi's travel-worn band wending its way down the pleasant valleys to the sea, one is moved to reflect that they have come an unconscionably long way just to build a ship. Well, let the reader suggest some other route. The best guide to Arabia at the time of the writing of the Book of Mormon imagined forests and lakes in the center of the peninsula, while insisting that the whole coastline was "a rocky wall . . . as dismal and barren as can be: not a blade of grass or a green thing," to be found.[20] The Book of Mormon reverses the picture and has Lehi avoid the heart of the continent to discover smiling woodlands on the south coast. Where else could he have found his timber on all the coast of Arabia? "It is quite probable," writes a present-day authority, "that Solomon has to transport his ships, or the material for them, from the Mediterranean, for where on the shores of the Red Sea could timber be found for ship-building?"[21]

And by what other route could Lehi have reached his happy shore? To the north lay enemy country, the Mediterranean was a world of closed harbors and closed seas, as dangerous as in the days of Wenamon, who was repeatedly stopped by enemies and pirates, the deserts to the east of Jerusalem swarmed with hostile and warring tribes, north and central Arabia were the classic grazing and fighting grounds of the Arabs, and so crisscrossed with trade routes in the time of Ptolemy "that there appears little left of the inaccessible desert: 'in general Ptolemy knows of no desert. . . .'"[22]

Egypt offered no escape to one marked as an enemy by the pro-Egyptian party. Only one way lay open, the hardest and wildest, through the mountains that border the Red Sea and then due east over the western extension of the terrible "Empty Quarter" where the party saw so much affliction. They had to turn east when they did because the whole southwest corner of the peninsula comprised the kingdom of the Sabaeans, probably the strongest, richest, and most thickly settled state Arabia has ever had.

So, long and painful though it was, Lehi's itinerary turns out to have been actually the shortest and safest, if not the only one he could have taken. On the shore of the Arabian Sea the story of Lehi in the Desert properly ends.

[15]*The Improvement Era*, vol. 53 (1950), p. 547.
[16]B. Thomas, *Arabia Felix*, pp. 48f.
[17]Burton, *Pilgrimage to Meccah*, II, 130, M.I.
[18]D. G. Hogarth, *Penetration of Arabia*, pp. 137ff, 148-150.
[19]J. A. Montgomery, *Arabia and the Bible*, pp. 71, 74.
[20]*Conder's Arabia* (The Modern Traveller Series, London, 1825), pp. 14f, 9, 348f.
[21]J. Perowne, in PEFQ [Palestine Exploration Fund Quarterly], 1939, p. 200.
[22]Montgomery, *Arabia and the Bible*, p. 75.

The Writings of Strabo

Appendix II

The following, an account (based on first-hand sources) of travel in Saudi Arabia in 24 B.C., is excerpted from The Geography of Strabo, *vol. 7 of seven volumes, translated from the Greek by Horace Leonard Jones (London: W. Heinemann Ltd., 1930), pp. 299-365.*

Strabo wrote of conditions in Arabia in the first century B.C., as well as the fascinating history of an ill-fated 10,000-man Roman infantry expedition to Arabia. This journey covered much of Lehi's trail, within six centuries of Lehi's time. Strabo of Amasia lived approximately 63 B.C. to A.D. 25. A Greek, he wrote seventeen books on geography, all published in 6 B.C.

Aelius Gallus was Strabo's "friend and companion" (2:5:12), the Roman Prefect of Egypt. Commanded by Emperor Caesar Augustus to reach and subjugate the incense country of Yemen and Dhofar (now in Oman), he took 10,000 infantry and landed, in 24 B.C., at Leucê Comê on the Red Sea coast in Arabia, a town on what is believed to be Lehi's trail. He then traveled down the eastern coast of the Red Sea along the frankincense trail, took the city of Najran near Abha, and laid siege to Marib, the capital of one of the new frankincense kingdoms. The siege was abandoned because of lack of water, and he then returned to Egypt after great loss of life. The account shows the difficulty and barrenness of part of the Lehi trail 572 years after Lehi had probably traveled there.

1. Above Judea and Coelê-Syria, as far as Babylonia and the river-country of the Euphrates towards the south, lies the whole of Arabia, . . . and of those parts that follow after Mesopotamia as far as Coelê-Syria, the part that lies near the river, as well as Mesopotamia, is occupied by Arabian Scenitae, who are divided off into small sovereignties and live in tracts that are barren for want of water. These people till the land either little or none, but they keep herds of all kinds, particularly of camels. Above these people lies an extensive desert; but the parts lying still farther south than their country are held by the people who inhabit Arabia Felix, as it is called. The northern side of Arabia Felix is formed by the above-mentioned desert, the eastern by the Persian Gulf, the western by the Arabian Gulf [Red Sea], and the southern by the great sea that lies outside both gulfs, which as a whole is called Erythra [Arabian Sea]. . . .

3. After sailing along the coast of Arabia for a distance of two thousand four hundred stadia [240 miles], one comes to Gerrha, a city situated on a deep gulf; it is inhabited by Chaldaeans, exiles from Babylon; the soil contains salt and the people live in houses made of salt; and since flakes of salt

continually scale off, owing to the scorching heat of the rays of the sun, and fall away, the people frequently sprinkle the houses with water and thus keep the walls firm. The city is two hundred stadia [twenty miles] distant from the sea; and the Garrhaeans traffic by land, for the most part, in the Arabian merchandise and aromatics, though Aristobulus says, on the contrary, that the Garrhaeans import most of their cargoes on rafts to Babylonia, and thence sail up the Euphrates with them, and then convey them by land to all parts of the country....

6. Along the whole of the coast of the Red Sea, down in the deep, grow trees [seaweed] like the laurel and the olive, which at the ebb tides are wholly visible above the water but at the full tides are sometimes wholly covered; and while this is the case, the land that lies above the sea has no trees, and therefore the peculiarity is all the greater. Such are the statements of Eratosthenes concerning the Persian Sea, which, as I was saying, forms the eastern side of Arabia Felix....

IV

4. Cattabania produces frankincense, and Chatramotitis produces myrrh; and both these and the other aromatics are bartered to merchants. These arrive there in seventy days from Aelana [Aqaba]....

21. The first people above Syria, who dwell in Arabia Felix are the Nabataeans and the Sabaeans. They often overran Syria before they became subject to the Romans; but at present both they and the Syrians are subject to the Romans. The metropolis of the Nabataeans is Petra, as it is called; for it lies on a site which is otherwise smooth and level, but it is fortified all round by a rock, the outside parts of the site being precipitous and sheer, and the inside parts having springs in abundance, both for domestic purposes and for watering gardens. Outside the circuit of the rock most of the territory is desert, in particular that towards Judaea. Here, too, is the shortest road to Hierecus [Jericho], a journey of three or four days, as also to the grove of palm trees, a journey of five days. Petra is always ruled by some king from the royal family; and the king has as Administrator one of his companions, who is called "brother." It is exceedingly well-governed; at any rate, Athenodorus, a philosopher and companion of mine, who had been in the city of the Petraeans, used to describe their government with admiration, for he said that he found both many Romans and many other foreigners sojourning there, and that he saw that the foreigners often engaged in lawsuits, both with one another and with the natives,

but that none of the natives prosecuted one another, and that they in every way kept peace with one another.

22. Many of the special characteristics of Arabia have been disclosed by the recent expedition of the Romans against the Arabians, which was made in my own time under Aelius Gallus as commander. He was sent by Augustus Caesar to explore the tribes and the places, not only in Arabia, but also in Aethiopia, since Caesar saw that the Troglodyte country which adjoins Aegypt neighbours upon Arabia, and also that the Arabian Gulf [Red Sea], which separates the Arabians from the Troglodytes, is extremely narrow. Accordingly he conceived the purpose of winning the Arabians over to himself or of subjugating them. Another consideration was the report, which had prevailed from all time, that they were very wealthy, and that they sold aromatics and the most valuable stones for gold and silver, but never expended with outsiders any part of what they received in exchange; for he expected either to deal with wealthy friends or to master wealthy enemies. He was encouraged also by the expectation of assistance from the Nabataeans, since they were friendly and promised to co-operate with him in every way.

23. Upon these considerations, therefore, Gallus set out on the expedition; but he was deceived by the Nabataean Administrator, Syllaeus, who, although he had promised to be guide on the march and to supply all needs and to co-operate with him, acted treacherously in all things, and pointed out neither a safe voyage along the coast nor a safe journey by land, misguiding him through places that had no roads and by circuitous routes and through regions destitute of everything, or along rocky shores that had no harbours or through waters that were shallow or full of submarine rocks; and particularly in places of that kind the flood-tides, as also the ebb-tides, caused very great distress. Now this was the first mistake of Gallus, to build long boats, since there was no naval war at hand, or even to be expected; for the Arabians are not very good warriors even on land, rather being hucksters and merchants, to say nothing of fighting at sea. But Gallus built not less than eighty boats, biremes and triremes and light boats, at Cleopatris [modern Suez City], which is near the old canal which extends [to the gulf] from the Nile. But when he realised that he had been thoroughly deceived, he built one hundred and thirty vessels of burden, on which he set sail with about ten thousand infantry, consisting of Romans in Aegypt, as also of Roman allies, among whom were five hundred Jews and one thousand Nabataeans under Syllaeus. After many experiences and hardships he arrived in fourteen days at Leucê Comê in the land of the

Nabataeans, a large emporium, although he had lost many of his boats, some of these being lost, crews and all, on account of difficult sailing, but not on account of any enemy. This was caused by the treachery of Syllaeus, who said that there was no way for an army to go to Leucê Comê by land; and yet camel-traders travel back and forth from Petra to this place in safety and ease, and in such numbers of men and camels that they differ in no respect from an army.

24. This came to pass because Obodas, the king, did not care much about public affairs, and particularly military affairs (this is a trait common to all the Arabian kings), and because he put everything in the power of Syllaeus; and because Syllaeus treacherously out-generalled Gallus in every way, and sought, as I think, to spy out the country and, along with the Romans, to destroy some of its cities and tribes, and then to establish himself lord of all after the Romans were wiped out by hunger and fatigue and diseases and any other evils which he had treacherously contrived for them. However, Gallus put in at Leucê Comê, his army now being sorely tried both with scurvy and with lameness in the leg, which are native ailments, the former disclosing a kind of paralysis round the mouth and the latter round the legs, both being the result of the native water and herbs. At all events, he was forced to spend both the summer and the winter there, waiting for the sick to recover. Now the loads of aromatics are conveyed from Leucê Comê to Petra, and thence to Rhinocolura, which is in Phoenicia near Aegypt, and thence to the other peoples; but at the present time they are for the most part transported by the Nile to Alexandria; and they are landed from Arabia and India at Myus Harbour; and then they are conveyed by camels over to Coptus in Thebaïs, which is situated on a canal of the Nile, and then to Alexandria. Again Gallus moved his army from Leucê Comê and marched through regions of such a kind that water had to be carried by camels, because of the baseness of the guides; and therefore it took many days to arrive at the land of Aretas, a kinsman of Obodas. Now Aretas received him in a friendly way and offered him gifts, but the treason of Syllaeus made difficult the journey through that country too; at any rate, it took thirty days to traverse the country, which afforded only zeia [a kind of coarse grain], a few palm trees, and butter instead of oil, because they passed through parts that had no roads. The next country which he traversed belonged to nomads and most of it was truly desert; and it was called Ararene; and its king was Sabos; and in passing through this country, through parts that had no roads, he spent fifty days, arriving at the city of the

Negrani [Najran] and at a country which was both peaceable and fertile. Now the king had fled and the city was seized at the first onset; and from there he arrived at the river in six days. Here the barbarians joined battle with the Romans, and about ten thousand of them fell, but only two Romans; for they used their weapons in an inexperienced manner, being utterly unfit for war, using bows and spears and swords and slings, though most of them used a double-edged axe; and immediately afterwards he took the city called Asca [site of the former Marib dam], which had been forsaken by its king; and thence he went to a city called Athrula; and, having mastered it without a struggle, he placed a garrison in it, arranged for supplies of grain and dates for his march, advanced to a city called Marsiaba [Marib], which belonged to the tribe of the Rhammanitae, who were subject to Ilasarus. Now he assaulted and besieged this city for six days, but for want of water desisted. He was indeed only a two days' journey from the country that produced aromatics, as informed by his captives, but he had used up six months' time on his marches because of bad guidance, and he realized the fact when he turned back, when at last he learned the plot against him and had gone back by other roads; for on the ninth day he arrived at Negrani [Najran] where the battle had taken place, and thence on the eleventh day at Hepta Phreata, as the place is called, from the fact that it has seven wells; and thence, at last, marching through a peaceable country, he arrived at a village called Chaalla, and again at another village called Malotha, which is situated near a river; and then through a desert country, which had only a few watering-places, as far as a village called Egra [Yenbo]. The village is in the territory of Obodas; and it is situated on the sea. On his return he accomplished the whole journey within sixty days, although he had used up six months in his first journey. Thence he carried his army across the Myus Harbour within eleven days, and marched by land over to Coptus, and, with all who had been fortunate enough to survive, landed at Alexandria. The rest he had lost, not in wars, but from sickness and fatigue and hunger and bad roads; for only seven men perished in war. For these reasons, also, this expedition did not profit us to a great extent in our knowledge of those regions, but still it made a slight contribution. But the man who was responsible for this failure, I mean Syllaeus, paid the penalty at Rome, since, although he pretended friendship, he was convicted, in addition to his rascality in this matter, of other offences too, and was beheaded.

25. Now writers divide the country that produces aromatics

into four parts, as I have said before; and, among the aromatics, they say that frankincense and myrrh are produced from trees and that cassia is produced also from marshes. Some say that most of the latter comes from India and that the best frankincense is produced near Persis. But, according to another division, Arabia Felix is split up into five kingdoms, one of which comprises the warriors, who fight for all; another, the farmers, who supply food to all the rest; another those who engage in the mechanical arts; another, the myrrh-bearing country, although the same countries produce cassia, cinnamon, and nard. Occupations are not changed from one class to another, but each and all keep to those of their fathers.

The Periplus of the Erythraean Sea

Appendix III

The following, the eye-witness account of a visit to several seaports along Lehi's probable trail over nineteen hundred years ago, is excerpted from The Periplus of the Erythraean Sea, Travel and Trade in the Indian Ocean by a Merchant of the First Century, *translated from the Greek by Wilfred H. Schoff (New Delhi: Oriental Books Reprint Corp., 1974), pp. 29-35, plus notes by Schoff.*

The unnamed author of the Periplus *was probably a Greek merchant of Alexandria, Egypt, who made the journey from Egypt through the Red Sea past ports on the Arabian peninsula, which would be close to Lehi's route. His course followed on to India about* A.D. *60. Some amazing details in the form of a nautical and commercial directory are contained in his record, which could qualify it as the original travel log. Though the author wrote about 660 years after Lehi's time, this account gives valuable insight into conditions as they probably existed in Lehi's day, since there was likely very little change until after Greek influence began to be felt there during the first century* A.D. *The western world learns here first of the regular monsoon winds that blow steadily from the southwest, beginning near the island of Madagascar, past Arabia, and across the Indian Ocean toward China, from June through November. Then, in amazing regularity even now, 2,000 years later, the following six months they blow in the opposite direction from the northeast. It is these same southwest monsoons that regularly water the Qara Mountains at Salalah, Dhofar, and nowhere else on the south Arabian shore. This southwest monsoon could have been utilized by Nephi to sail eastward toward China to a point where he could have picked up ocean currents to carry his colony to America.*

19. Now to the left of Berenice [that is, on the east shore of the Red Sea], sailing for two or three days from Mussel Harbor [Egypt] eastward across the adjacent gulf [of the Red Sea] there is another harbor and fortified place, which is called White Village [Leucê Comê] from which there is a road to Petra, which is subject to Malichas, King of the Nabataeans. It holds the position of a market-town for the small vessels sent there from Arabia; and so a centurion is stationed there as a collector of one-fourth of the merchandise imported, with an armed force, as a garrison.

NOTES: *White Village* (Leucê Comê) is placed by most commentators at El Haura, . . . which lies in a bay protected by Hasani island. The name *Haura* also means "white," and the Arab name itself appears as *Auara*, in Ptolemy. The place is on the regular caravan route that led, and still leads, from Aden to the Mediterranean.

Small vessels from Arabia.—Strabo (XVI, IV, 24) has the following account of this trade:

"Merchandise is conveyed from Leucê Comê to Petra, thence to Rhinocolura in Phoenicia near Egypt, and thence to other nations. But at present the greater part is transported by the Nile to Alexandria. It is brought from Arabia and India to Myos Hormus, and is then conveyed on camels to Coptus of the Thebais, situated on a canal of the Nile, and to Alexandria."

The policy of the Ptolemies, in seeking to free Egypt from commercial dependence on Yemen, and to encourage direct communication with India, had been continued by Rome at the expense of the Arabs. The "small vessels" of para. 19 from Muza to the Nabataean port are to be contrasted with the "large vessels" of para. 10 that traded from Mosyllum to Egypt. The caravan trade could not be reached in the same way, and along the Red Sea the camel could always compete with the ship. This remained in Arabian hands for another half-century, when the Emperor Trajan reduced the Nabataeans to subjection to Rome.

20. Directly below this place is the adjoining country of Arabia, in its length bordering a great distance on the Erythraean Sea. Different tribes inhabit the country, differing in their speech, some partially, and some altogether. The land next the sea is similarly dotted here and there with caves of the Fish-Eaters, but the country inland is peopled by rascally men speaking two languages, who live in villages and nomadic camps, by whom those sailing off the middle course are plundered, and those surviving shipwrecks are taken for slaves. And so they too are continually taken prisoners by the chiefs and kings of Arabia; and they are called Carnaites. Navigation is dangerous along this whole coast of Arabia, which is without harbors, with bad anchorages, foul, inaccessible because of breakers and rocks, and terrible in every way. Therefore we hold our course down the middle of the gulf and pass on as fast as possible by the country of Arabia until we come to the Burnt Island; directly below which there are regions of peaceful people, nomadic, pasturers of cattle, sheep and camels.

NOTES: 20. Carnaites.—Pliny (VI, 32) and Ptolemy both mention [Karna] as a city of the Minaeans; whom Pliny describes as the oldest commercial people in Arabia, having a monopoly in the trade in myrrh and frankincense, through their control of the caravan-routes from the producing regions. He refers doubtfully to their legend of the relationship of Minaeans and Rhadamaeans to Minos of Crete and his brother

Rhadamanthus. Pliny need not have doubted, and is to be thanked for preserving this evidence of early Arabian trade in the Mediterranean. Ptolemy adds his testimony to the wide extent of this early Arabian trade, when he describes the "people called Rhamnae who dwelt in the extreme east near the banks of the Purali, and who planted their capital at a place called Rhambacia." From Crete to the borders of India was no mean sphere of activity. Compare Ezekiel XXVII, 22: "The merchants of Sheba and Raamah, they were thy merchants: They occupied in thy fairs with chief of all spices, and with all precious stones, and gold."

Strabo also (XVI, III, I) describes "the Minaei in the part toward the Red Sea, whose largest city is Carna; next to them are the Sabaeans, whose chief city is Mariaba."

At the time of the Periplus the term "Minaean" was no longer limited to the southern traders, but had been extended to include the nomadic Ishmaelites over whom their settlements along the caravan-routes exerted a varying measure of authority.

The Minaean kingdom had long since lost its identity, having been conquered by the Sabaeans. When Saba fell before Himyar its allegiance was transferred likewise; but we may assume that at the date of the Periplus it was almost independent. When the Homerite dynasty became powerful, it asserted its authority over most of the Hejaz; when the Abyssinians conquered Yemen their rule was not acknowledged so far north. The insurgence of the Ishmaelites under the spur of Islam was a logical consequence of centuries of civil war among their former overlords in Yemen.

21. Beyond these places, in a bay at the foot of the left side of this gulf, there is a place by the shore called Muza, a market-town established by law, distant altogether from Berenice for those sailing southward, about twelve thousand stadia [1200 miles]. And the whole place is crowded with Arab shipowners and seafaring men, and is busy with the affairs of commerce; for they carry on a trade with the far-side coast and with Barygaza, sending their own ships there.

22. Three days inland from this port there is a city called Saua, in the midst of the region called Mapharitis; and there is a vassal-chief named Cholaebus who lives in that city.

23. And after nine days more there is Saphar, the metropolis, in which lives Charibael, lawful king of two tribes, the Homerites and those living next to them, called the Sabaites; through continual embassies and gifts, he is a friend of the Emperors.

NOTES: *Homerites and Sabaites.*—Both were of the Joktan-ite race of South Arabia, the former being the younger branch. In the tribal genealogy in Genesis X, we are shown their relation to the Semites of the North. Three of the children of Shem are given as Elam, Asshur, and Arphaxad. Arphaxad's son was Salah, and his grandson Eber. These names are associated with Babylonia and Chaldaea. Eber's second son was Joktan, of which the Arabic form is Kahtan, which appears farther south along the Persian Gulf, in the peninsula of El Katan. Of the sons of Joktan, most are identified with the southern coast; two of them being Hasarmaveth (Hadramaut), and Jerah (*cf.* the *Jerakôn Komê* of Ptolemy, north of Dhofar). The last-named the Arabs call Yarab: his son was Yashab (*cf.* the Asabi in Oman, para. 35), and his grandson "Saba the Great" (surnamed Abd-es-Shems) is said to have founded the city of Marib, and to have begun its great dam, on which the irrigation of the vicinity depended. The Sabaeans are thus connected with this Saba, a descendant of Jerah, and not with Sheba, son of Joktan, who is referred rather to Central Arabia; whom Glaser and Hommel would make a colony from Yemen, while Weber would reverse the process, having the Sabaeans migrate southward for the conquest of the Minaeans.

According to Arab accounts the dam at Marib was finished by a certain King Zul Karnain, suggesting the primacy of the Minaean dynasty at that time; but from about the 7th century B.C. the Sabaeans were supreme in all southern Arabia, controlling the caravan-routes, and forcing the wild tribes into caravan service. Colonies and resting-stations were established at intervals along the routes. We learn from the Koran (Chap. XXXIV) that the journey was easy between these cities, and travel secure by night or by day; the distances being so short that the heat of the day might be passed in one, and the night in the next, so that provisions need not be carried. The number of such settlements may be inferred from Strabo's statement that the caravans took seventy days between Minaea and Aelana; and all the Greek and Roman writers, from Eratosthenes to Pliny, testify to the value of the trade, the wealth of those who controlled it, and their jealous hindrance of all competition.

The entry of the fleets of the Ptolemies into the Red Sea, and their establishment of colonies along its shores, dealt a hard blow to the caravan-trade. If we sift fact from homily in the same chapter of the Koran, we find that the result was abandonment of many of the caravan-stations, and a consequent increase in the cost of camel-hire and of the provisions which now had to be carried; impoverishment, dispersion and rebellion of the swellers in the stations, so that finally "most of the cities which were between Saba and Syria were ruined and abandoned," and a few years later than the Periplus, Marib itself, stripped of its revenues and unable to maintain its public works, was visited with an inundation which carried away its famous reservoir-dam, making the city uninhabitable and forcing the dispersion of its people. Many of them seem to have migrated northward and to have settled in the country southeast of Judaea, founding the kingdom of the Ghassanids, which was for generations a bulwark of the Roman Empire at its eastern boundary.

The great expedition against Sabaea by the Romans under Aelius Gallus, (Strabo, XVI, IV, 22-4; Pliny, VI, 32) never got beyond the valley of the Minaeans; turning back thence, as Vincent surmised (II, 306-311), and as Glaser proves (*Skizze,* 56-9), without reaching Marib, and probably without inflicting any lasting injury on the tribes along their route. It was the merchant-shipping of the Romans, and not their soldiery, that undermined the power of the Sabaeans.

As the wealth of Marib declined, its power was resolved into its elements, and was reorganized by a neighbor of the same blood. The oldest son of Saba the Great, founder of Marib, was Himyar, whose descendants included most of the town-folk of the southwest corner of Arabia. Two sons of Himyar, Malik and Arib, had carried the Joktanite arms back toward the east again, subduing the earlier inhabitants of the frankincense region north of Dhofar. The center of the tribe was at Zafar, southwest of Marib, and some days' journey nearer the sea. Allied with the sheikh at Zafar was he of the Ma'afir, controlling the port of Muza. This combination was able to overthrow the old order, Zafar supplanting Marib, and Muza stripping Aden of its trade and its privileges along the African coast. Thereafter the Himyarite dynasty—the Homerite kings—assumed the title "Kings of Saba and Raidan." This was during the first century B.C.

24. The market-town of Muza is without a harbor, but has a good roadstead and anchorage because of the sandy bottom thereabouts, where the anchors hold safely. The merchandise imported there consists of purple cloths, both fine and coarse; clothing in the Arabian style, with sleeves; plain, ordinary, embroidered, or interwoven with gold; saffron, sweet rush, muslins, cloaks, blankets (not many), some plain and others made in the local fashion; sashes of different colors, fragrant ointments in moderate quantity, wine and wheat, not much. For the country produces grain in moderate amount, and a great

deal of wine. And to the King and the Chief are given horses and sumpter-mules, vessels of gold and polished silver, finely woven clothing and copper vessels. There are exported from the same place the things produced in the country: selected myrrh, and the Gebanite-Minaean *stacte*, alabaster and all the things already mentioned from Avalites and the far-side coast. The voyage to this place is made best about the month of September, that is Thoth; but there is nothing to prevent it even earlier.

25. After sailing beyond this place about three hundred stadia [30 miles], the coast of Arabia and the Berber country about the Avalitic gulf now coming close together, there is a channel, not long in extent, which forces the sea together and shuts it into a narrow strait, the passage through which, sixty stadia in length, the island Diodorus divides. Therefore the course through it is beset with rushing currents and with strong winds blowing down from the adjacent ridge of mountains. Directly on this strait by the shore there is a village of Arabs, subject to the same chief, called Ocelis; which is not so much a market-town as it is an anchorage and watering-place and the first landing for those sailing into the gulf.

26. Beyond Ocelis, the sea widening again toward the east and soon giving a view of the open ocean, after about twelve hundred stadia there is Eudaemon Arabia [Aden], a village by the shore, also of the Kingdom of Charibael, and having convenient anchorages, and watering-places, sweeter and better than those at Ocelis; it lies at the entrance of a bay, and the land recedes from it. It was called Eudaemon, because in the early days of the city when the voyage was not yet made from India to Egypt, and when they did not dare to sail from Egypt to the ports across this ocean, but all came together at this place, it received the cargoes from both countries, just as Alexandria now receives the things brought both from abroad and from Egypt. But not long before our own time Charibael destroyed the place.

27. After Eudaemon Arabia there is a continuous length of coast, and a bay extending two thousand stadia or more, along which there are Nomads and Fish-Eaters living in villages; just beyond the cape projecting from this bay there is another market-town by the shore, Cana, of the Kingdom of Eleazus, the Frankincense Country; and facing it there are two desert islands, one called Island of birds, the other Dome Island, one hundred and twenty stadia from Cana. Inland from this place lies the metropolis Sabbatha, in which the King lives. All the frankincense produced in the country is brought by camels to

that place to be stored, and to Cana on rafts held up by inflated skins after the manner of the country, and in boats. And this place has a trade also with the farside ports, with Barygaza and Scythia and Ommana and the neighboring coast of Persia.

NOTES: *Eleazus, King of the Frankincense Country.*—This is the Arabic Ili-azzu, "my God is mighty," a name which Glaser shows to have belonged to several kings of the Hadramaut; and this Eleazus he identifies with Ili-azzu Jalit, of whose reign, dating about 25-65 A.D., he gives an inscription *(Die Abessinier,* 34, etc.).

The name given the kingdom, "Frankincense Country," is notable, being a translation of the "Incense-Land" of the Habashat, or Aethiopians, already mentioned. This ancient object of contention among the nations was now divided between Hadramaut and Parthia, and its name was, apparently, assumed by the king of the Hadramaut; perhaps officially, but certainly by the popular voice, and by merchants such as the author of the Periplus, interested in the product of the country and not in its politics.

A glance at the topography of this Incense-Land will help toward an understanding of its dealings with its neighbors. The southern coast of Arabia from Bab el Mandeb to Ras el Hadd has a length of about 1200 miles, divided almost equally in climatic conditions. The western half is largely sandstone bluff, sun-scorched and arid; cut, however, by occasional ravines which bring down scanty rains during the monsoon to fertilize a broad strip of coast plain. On the western edge the mountains of Yemen, rising above 10,000 feet, attract a good rainfall which waters the western slope toward the Red Sea. On the eastern slope the watercourses are soon lost in the sand, but on the upper levels the valleys are protected and fertile. Such were the Nejran, the Minaean Jauf, and the valley of the Sabaeans, which last was made rich by the great dam that stored its waters for irrigation; and these three valleys, the centers of caravan-trade bound north toward the Nile and Euphrates, owed their prosperity mainly to their position above the greatest of all the east-flowing courses, the Valley of Hadramaut. This great cleft in the sandstone rock, (originally, Bent believes, an arm of the sea, now silted up), which gathers the streams from the highest peaks, runs parallel with the coast for more than 200 miles, fertile and productive for nearly the entire distance; then it turns to the south and its waters are lost, the mouth of the valley being desert like the cliffs that line its course. This was one of the best frankincense districts.

Beyond the mouth of the Wadi Hadramaut is Ras Fartak,

nearly north of Cape Guardafui. Here the climate changes; the monsoon no longer checked by the African coast, leaves its effect on the coastal hills, which gradually rise above 4000 feet, clothed with tropical vegetation; while the coast plains are narrow and broken. The northern slopes of these mountains (known to our author as Asich, para. 33) feed the watercourse now known as the Wadi Rekot, about 100 miles long, which empties into the Kuria Muria Bay; beyond which are fertile coast plains as far as Ras el Hadd. These mountains, and the Dhofar mountains, the Hadramaut valley, and the opposite Somali coast of Africa—thus controlling the production and commanding the price; in short, forming a "frankincense trust." The restricted area of the Arabian incense-lands, bordered as they were by the steppe and the desert, made them constantly subject to attack and control by different wandering tribes; while at the same time their local conditions, of intensive cultivation of a controlled product of great and constant value, made for a peculiarly ordered state of society—for a development of caste unusual in Semitic lands, and in which the cultivator, the warrior, and the privileged slave, had their place in the order given.

Of the age-long struggle for control of these sacred lands we know today little more than the Greek writers of two thousand years ago. The modern world takes its little supply of frankincense from the Arab vessels that carry it to Bombay or Aden; its armies are sent to the conquest or defence of lands in other lines of productivity—of a Kimberley, a Witwatersrand, a Manchuria. But to the ancient world the Incense-Land was a true Eldorado, sought by the great empires and fought for by every Arab tribe that managed to enrich itself by trading incense for temple-service on the Nile or Euphrates, on Mount Zion, or in Persia, India, or China. The archaeological expedition that shall finally succeed in penetrating these forbidden regions, and recovering the records of their past, cannot fail to add greatly to our store of knowledge of the surrounding civilizations, by showing the complement to such records as those of Hatshepsut in Egypt and Tiglath-Pileser III in Assyria, and by giving the groundwork for the treasured scraps of information preserved by Herodotus, Theophrastus, Eratosthenes, Agatharchides, Strabo, Pliny, and Ptolemy. At present we must be satisfied with such knowledge of the Incense-Land as may be had from these, and from inscriptions found by Halévy and Glaser in the homes of its neighbors, the Minaeans and Sabaeans.

Frankincense, one of the most ancient and precious articles of commerce, is a resin exuded from various species of *Boswellia,* order *Burseraceae,* native in Somaliland and South Arabia. Birdwood *(Trans. Linn Soc.,* XXVII, 1871), distinguishes particularly *B. Frereana, B. Bhau-Dajiana* (the *mocrotu* of para. 9), and *B. Carteru,* the last-named yielding the best incense. *B. thurifera,* native in India, yields a resin of less fragrance, much used as an adulterant. Frankincense is thus closely allied to myrrh, bdellium, and benzoin.

The Greek word is *libanos,* from Hebrew *Lebonah,* Arabic *lubân,* meaning "white;" *cf. laben,* the Somali word for cream, and "milk-perfume," which is the Chinese term for frankincense. Marco Polo always calls it "white incense."

Another Hebrew name was *shekheleth,* Ethiopic *sekhin,* which Hommel would connect with the "Bay of Sachalites" of para. 29.

The inscriptions of the early Egyptian dynasties contain, as we might expect, few references to the trade in incense, which was brought overland to the upper Nile by the "people of Punt and God's Land" and not sought out by the Pharaohs. That incense was in use is sufficiently clear from the early ritual. The expedition to the Incense-Land under Sahure, in the Vth dynasty (28th century B.C.) was a notable exception. In the VIth dynasty, under Pepi II (26th century B.C.), a royal officer Sebni, sent to the Tigre highlands, records how he "descended to Wawat and Uthek, and sent on the royal attendant Iri, with two others, bearing incense, clothing [probably cotton], one tusk, and one hide" (as specimens). In the XIth dynasty, under Mentuhotep IV (21st century B.C.), a record of the completion of a royal sarcophagus states that "Cattle were slaughtered, goats were slain, incense was put on the fire. Behold, an army of 3000 sailors of the nomes of the Northland [Delta of the Nile] followed it in safety to Egypt." And in the XIIth dynasty, under Amenemhet I (20th century B.C.), another royal officer named Intef was sent for to Hammamat along what was, in the time of the Periplus, the caravan-route from Coptos to Berenice. He sought for it eight days without success, then prostrated himself "to Min, to Mut, to—Great-in-Magic, and all the gods of this highland, giving to them incense upon the fire. . . . Then all scattered in search, and I found it, and the entire army was praising, it rejoiced with obeisance; I gave praise to Montu."

Then followed a period of disorder and Arabian domination in Egypt, during which Arab merchants controlled the trade. This was the condition described in Genesis XXXVII, 25, when "a traveling company of Ishmaelites came from Gilead, with their camels bearing spicery and balm and myrrh, going to carry it down to Egypt." It was ended by a native reaction under the great Pharaohs of the XVIIIth or Theban dynasty, under whom the land increased in power in all directions. These monarchs were not content to remain in commercial dependence upon Arabia, but organized great fleets which went to the "Land of Punt" each season and brought back unprecedented treasure. This land in former times, according to the Deir el Bahri reliefs, "the people knew not; it was heard of from mouth to mouth by hearsay of the ancestors. The marvels brought thence under thy fathers, the kings of Lower Egypt, were brought from one to another, and since the time of the ancestors of the kings of Upper Egypt, who were of old, as a return for many payments; none reaching them except thy carriers." But Amon-Re, so the inscription continues, led the Egyptian army by land and sea, until it came to the Incense-Land, and brought back great store of myrrh, ebony and ivory, gold, cinnamon, incense, eye-paint, apes, monkeys, dogs, panther-skins, natives and their children. "Never was brought the like of this for any king who has been since the beginning." Incense-trees were planted in the court of the temple; "heaven and earth are flooded with incense; odors are in the Great House," and the heart of Amon was made glad.

Then followed a series of campaigns in Syria, resulting in the submission of that country, and annual remittances of great quantities of Arabian and Eastern treasure—incense, oil, grain, wine, gold and silver, precious stones—while even the "Chief of Shinar" at Babylon sent gifts of lapis lazuli, and the "Genabti" of the Incense-Land came direct, offering their tribute. The sudden opulence of the Theban dynasty made possible a great enrichment in the worship of Amon, and the setting aside of enormous endowments for the temples, as well as annual gifts of princely value. So Rameses II, of the XIXth dynasty (1292-1225 B.C), "founded for his father offerings for his *ka*—wine, incense, all fruit, cultivated trees, growing for him;" while the court responded that Rameses himself was "the god of all people, that they may awake, to give to thee incense." His successor Merneptah was bidden by the All-Lord to "set free multitudes who are bound in every district, to give offerings to the temples, to send in incense before the god." And in the XXth dynasty, under Rameses III (1198-1167 B.C.), it seemed as if the resources of the nation were poured bodily into the lap of Amon. The god opened for the Pharaoh "the ways of Punt, with myrrh and incense for thy serpent diadem;" "the Sand-Dwellers came bowing down to thy name." And in the *Papyrus Harris,* that great record of his gifts and endowments to Amon, compiled for his tomb, there are such entries every year as "gold, silver, lapis lazuli, malachite, precious stones, copper, garments of royal linen, jars, fowl; myrrh, 21,140 *deben,* white incense 2,159 jars, cinnamon 246 measures, incense 304,093 various measures;" stored of necessity, in a special "Incense House." (The quotations are from Breasted, *Ancient Records of Egypt.)*

28. There are imported into this place from Egypt a little wheat and wine, as at Muza; clothing in the Arabian style, plain and common and most of it spurious; and copper and tin and coral and storax and other things such as go to Muza; and for the King usually wrought gold and silver plate, also horses, images, and thin clothing of fine quality. And there are exported from this place, native produce, frankincense and aloes, and the rest of the things that enter into the trade of the other ports. The voyage to this place is best made at the same time as that to Muza, or rather earlier.

29. Beyond Cana, the land receding greatly, there follows a very deep bay stretching a great way across, which is called Sachalites; and the Frankincense Country, mountainous and forbidding, wrapped in thick clouds and fog, and yielding frankincense from the trees. These incense-bearing trees are not of great height or thickness; they bear the frankincense sticking in drops on the bark, just as the trees among us in Egypt weep their gum. The frankincense is gathered by the King's slaves and those who are sent to this service for punishment. For these places are very unhealthy, and pestilential even to those sailing along the coast; but almost always fatal to those working there, who also perish often from want of food.

30. On this bay there is a very great promontory facing the east, called Syagrus; on which is a fort for the defence of the country, and a harbor and storehouse for the frankincense that is collected, and opposite this cape, well out at sea, there is an island, lying between it and the Cape of Spices opposite, but nearer Syagrus: it is called Dioscorida, and is very large but desert and marshy, having rivers in it and crocodiles and many snakes and great lizards, of which the flesh is eaten and the fat melted and used instead of olive oil. The island yields no fruit, neither vine nor grain. The inhabitants are few and they live on the coast toward the north, which from this side faces the continent. They are foreigners, a mixture of Arabs and Indians and Greeks, who have emigrated to carry on trade there. The island produces the true sea-tortoise, and the land-tortoise, and the white tortoise which is very numerous and preferred for its large shells; and the mountain-tortoise, which is largest of all

and has the thickest shell; of which the worthless specimens cannot be cut apart on the under side, because they are even too hard; but those of value are cut apart and the shells made whole into caskets and small plates and cake-dishes and that sort of ware. There is also produced in this island cinnabar, that called Indian, which is collected in drops from the trees.

31. It happens that just as Azania is subject to Charibael and the Chief of Mapharitis, this island is subject to the King of the Frankincense Country. Trade is also carried on there by some people from Muza and by those who chance to call thereon the voyage from Damirica and Barygaza; they bring in rice and wheat and Indian cloth, and a few female slaves; and they take for their exchange cargoes, a great quantity of tortoise-shell. Now the island is farmed out under the Kings and is garrisoned.

32. Immediately beyond Syagrus the bay of Omana cuts deep into the coast-line, the width of it being six hundred stadia [60 miles]; and beyond this there are mountains, high and rocky and steep, inhabited by cave-dwellers for five hundred stadia more; and beyond this is a port established for receiving the Sachalitic frankincense; the harbor is called Moscha [Salalah, Dhofar], and ships from Cana call there regularly; and ships returning from Damirica [India] and Barygaza, if the season is late, winter there, and trade with the King's officers, exchanging their cloth and wheat and sesame oil for frankincense, which lies in heaps all over the Sachalitic country, open and unguarded, as if the place were under the protection of the gods; for neither openly nor by stealth can it be loaded on board ship without the King's permission; if a single grain were loaded without this, the ship could not clear from the harbor.

The Writings of Pliny

Appendix IV

The following, an account of the possible route Lehi took two thousand years ago, is taken from Pliny, Natural History, *translated from the Latin by H. Rackham (London: William Heinemann Ltd., 1952), pp. 37-63.*

Pliny the Elder lived about 23 B.C. *to* A.D. *79 in the Roman province of Gaul (now France). He was on intimate terms with the Roman Emperor Vesparian. His celebrated literary work* Natural History *in thirty-seven books has been criticized as being unscientific and uncritical but it is nevertheless a valuable window for modern man to view many details of civilization two thousand years ago. In Book 12, Pliny tells how merchants could travel from Egypt to Arabia and India and return with a cargo in one year and gives much information about production and trade of frankincense. His comments on Arabs and Arabia are enlightening since they were written, though 600 years from Lehi's time, within the first century of Greek contact and influence with the area—the first major factor for change since Lehi. Pliny's account also provides important confirmation of the description of Arabia in* The Periplus *(Appendix III).*

Section VI:26

In later times it has been considered a well-ascertained fact that the voyage from Syagrus, the Promontory of Arabia, to Patala, reckoned at thirteen hundred and thirty-five miles, can be performed most advantageously with the aid of a westerly wind, which is there known by the name of Hippalus.

The age that followed pointed out a shorter route, and a safer one to those who might happen to sail from the same promontory for Sigerus, a port in India, and for a long time this route was followed, until at last a still shorter cut was discovered by a merchant, and the thirst for gain brought India even still nearer to us. At the present day voyages are made to India every year; and companies of archers are carried on board the vessels, as those seas are greatly infested with pirates.

It will not be amiss too, on the present occasion, to set forth the whole of the route from Egypt, which has been stated to us of late, upon information on which reliance may be placed, and is here published for the first time. The subject is one well worthy of our notice, seeing that in no year does India drain our empire of less than five hundred and fifty millions of sesterces, giving back her own wares in exchange, which are sold among us at fully one hundred times their prime cost.

Two miles distant from Alexandria is the town of Juliopolis. The distance thence to Coptos, up the Nile, is three hundred and eight miles; the voyage is performed, when the Etesian winds are blowing, in twelve days. From Coptos the journey is made with the aid of camels, stations being arranged at intervals for the supply of fresh water. The first of these stations is called Hydreuma (watering-place), and is distant twenty-two miles; the second is situated on a mountain, at a distance of one day's journey from the last; the third is at a second Hydreuma distant from Coptos ninety-five miles; the fourth is on a mountain; the next to that is another Hydreuma, that of Apollo, and is distant from Coptos one hundred and eighty-four miles; after which, there is another on a mountain. There is then another station at a place called the New Hydreuma, distant from Coptos two hundred and thirty miles; and next to it there is another, called the Old Hydreuma, or the Troglodytic, where a detachment is always on guard, with a caravansary that affords lodging for two thousand persons. This last is distant from the New Hydreuma seven miles. After leaving it we come to the city of Berenice, situated upon a harbor of the Red Sea and distant from Coptos two hundred and fifty-seven miles. The greater part of this distance is generally travelled by night, on account of the extreme heat, the days being spent at the stations; in consequence of which it takes twelve days to perform the whole journey from Coptos to Berenice.

Passengers generally set sail at midsummer, before the rising of the Dog-star, or else immediately after, and in about thirty days arrive at Ocelis in Arabia, or else at Cana, in the region which bears frankincense. There is also a third port of Arabia, Muza by name; it is not, however, used by persons on their passage to India, as only those touch at it who deal in incense and the perfumes of Arabia. More in the interior there is a city; the residence of the king there is called Sapphar, and there is another city known by the name of Save. To those who are bound for India, Ocelis is the best place for embarcation. If the wind, called Hippalus, happens to be blowing, it is possible to arrive in forty days at the nearest mart in India, Muziris by name. This, however, is not a very desirable place for disembarcation, on account of the pirates which frequent its vicinity, where they occupy a place called Nitrias; nor, in fact, is it very rich in articles of merchandise. Besides, the roadstead for shipping is a considerable distance from the shore, and the cargoes have to be conveyed in boats, either for loading or discharging. At the moment that I am writing these pages, the name of the king of this place is Caelobothras. Another port, and a much more convenient one, is that which lies in the territory of the people called Neacyndi, Barace by name. Here king Pandion used to reign, dwelling at a considerable distance from the mart in the interior, at a city known as Modiera. The district from which pepper is carried down to Barace in boats hollowed out of a single tree is known as Cottonara. None of these names of nations, ports and cities are to be found in any of the former writers, from which circumstance it would appear that the localities have since changed their names. Travellers set sail from India on their return to Europe, at the beginning of the Egyptian month of Tybis, which is our December, or at all events before the sixth day of the Egyptian month Mechir, the same as our Ides of January; if they do this they can go and return in the same year. They set sail from India with a south-east wind, and upon entering the Red Sea, catch the south-west or south.

Section XXX:53

Next in affinity to cardamomum would have come cinnamomum, were it not convenient first to catalogue the riches of Arabia and the reasons that have given it the names of Happy and Blessed. The chief products of Arabia then are frankincense and myrrh; the latter it shares also with the Cave-dwellers' Country, but no country beside Arabia produces frankincense, and not even the whole of Arabia. About in the middle of that country are the Astramitae, a district of the Sabaei, the capital of their realm being Sabota, situated on a lofty mountain; and eight days' journey from Sabota is a frankincense-producing district belonging to the Sabaei called Sariba—according to the Greeks the name means "secret mystery." The region faces north-east, and is surrounded by impenetrable rocks, and on the right hand side bordered by a seacoast with inaccessible cliffs. The soil is reported to be of a milky white colour with a tinge of red. . . . There are hills rising to a great height, with natural forests on them running right down to the level ground. It is generally agreed that the soil is clay, and that there are a few springs and these charred with alkali. Adjacent to the Astramitae is another district, the Minaci, through whose territory the transit for the export of the frankincense is along one narrow track. It was these people who originated the trade and who chiefly practice it, and from them the perfume takes the name of "Minaean"; none of the Arabs beside these have ever seen an incense-tree, and not even all of these, and it is said that there are not more than 3000 families who retain the right of trading in it as a hereditary property, and that consequently the members of these families are called sacred, and are not allowed to be polluted by ever meeting women or funeral processions when they are engaged in making incisions in the trees in order to obtain the frankincense, and that in this way the price of the commodity is increased owing to scruples of religion. Some persons report that the frankincense in the forests belongs to all these peoples in common, but others state that it is shared out among them in yearly turns. . . .

XXXII. It used to be the custom, when there were fewer opportunities of selling frankincense, to gather it only once a year, but at the present day trade introduces a second harvesting. The earlier and natural gathering takes place at about the rising of the Dogstar, when the summer heat is most intense. They make an incision where the bark appears to be fullest of juice and distended to its thinnest; and the bark is loosened with a blow, but not removed. From the incision a greasy foam spurts out, which coagulates and thickens, being received on a mat of palm-leaves where the nature of the ground requires this, but in other places on a space round the tree that has been rammed hard. The frainkincense collected in the latter way is in a purer state, but the former method produces a heavier weight; while the residue adhering to the tree is scraped off with an iron tool, and consequently contains fragments of bark. The forest is divided up into definite portions, and owing to the mutual honesty of the owners is free from trespassing, and though nobody keeps guard over the trees after an incision has been made, nobody steals from his neighbour. At Alexandria, on the other hand, where the frankincense is worked up for sale, good heavens! no vigilance is sufficient to guard the factories. A seal is put upon the workmen's aprons, they have to wear a mask or a net with a close mesh on their heads, and before they are allowed to leave the premises they have to take off all their clothes: so much less honesty is displayed with regard to the produce with them than as to the forests with the growers. The frankincense from the summer crop is collected in autumn; this is the purest kind, bright white in colour. The second crop is harvested in the spring, cuts having been made in the bark during the winter in preparation for it; the juice that comes out on this occasion is reddish, and not to be compared with the former taking, the name for which is carfiathum, the other being called dathiathum. Also the juice produced by a sapling is believed to be whiter, but that from an older tree has more scent. Some people also think that a better kind is produced on islands, but Juba says that no incense grows on islands at all.

Frankincense that hangs suspended in a globular drop we call male frankincense. . . . The Greek name for frankincense formed in this manner is "drop-incense" or "solid incense," and for the smaller kind "chick-pea incense"; the fragments knocked off by striking the tree we call manna. Even at the present day, however, drops are found that weigh as much as a third of a mina, that is 28 denarii [about a third of a pound]. Alexander the Great in his boyhood was heaping frankincense on the altars in lavish fashion, when his tutor Leonides told him that he might worship the gods in that manner when he had conquered the frankincense-producing races; but when Alexander had won Arabia he sent Leonides a ship with a cargo of frankincense, with a message charging him to worship the gods without any stint.

Frankincense after being collected is conveyed to Sabota on camels, one of the gates of the city being opened for its admission; the kings have made it a capital offence for camels so laden to turn aside from the high road. At Sabota a tithe estimated by measure and not by weight is taken by the priests for the god they call Sabis, and the incense is not allowed to be put on the market until this has been done; this tithe is drawn on to defray what is a public expenditure, for actually on a fixed number of days the god graciously entertains guests at a banquet. It can only be exported through the country of the Gebbanitae, and accordingly a tax is paid on it to the king of that people as well. Their capital is Thomna, which is 1487½ miles distant from the town of Gaza in Judaea on the Mediterranean coast; the journey is divided into 65 stages with halts for camels. Fixed portions of the frankincense are also given to the priests and the king's secretaries, but beside these guards and their attendants and the gate-keepers and servants also have their pickings: indeed all along the route they keep on paying, at one place for water, at another for fodder, or the charges for lodging at the halts, and the various octrois; so that expenses mount up to 688 denarii per camel before the Mediterranean coast is reached; and then again payment is made to the customs officers of our empire. Consequently the price of the best frankincense is 6, of the second best 5, and third best 3 denarii a pound. It is tested by its whiteness and stickiness, its fragility and its readiness to catch fire from a hot coal; and also it should not give to pressure of the teeth, and should rather crumble into grains. Among us it is adulterated with drops of white resin, which closely resemble it, but the fraud can be detected by the means specified. . . .

XL. They also import from Carmania the stobrus tree, to use for the purpose of fumigation; it is soaked in palm wine and then set alight. The vapour is thrown back from the ceiling to the floor; it has an agreeable scent, but it causes headache, which is not however severe enough to be painful: it is used as a soporific for invalids. For these trades they have opened up the city of Carrhae, which is the market town of these parts. From Carrhae everybody used formerly to go on to Gabba, a journey of twenty days, and to Palestine in Syria; but afterwards, according to Juba, they began to make for Charax and the Parthian kingdom for the sake of the perfume trade. But my own view is that they used to convey those commodities to the Persians even before they took them to Syria or Egypt, this being attested by Herodotus, who records that the Arabs used regularly to pay a yearly tribute of a thousand talents of incense to the kings of the Persians. From Syria they bring back styrax, which they burn on their hearths, for its powerful scent to dispel their dislike for their own scents. For the rest, no other kinds of wood are in use among them except those that are scented; and the Sabaei even cook their food with incensewood, and other tribes with that of the myrrh-tree, so that the smoke and vapour of their towns and districts is just like that which rises from altars. In order therefore to remedy this smell they obtain styrax in goat-skins and fumigate their houses with it: so true it is that there is no pleasure the continued enjoyment of which does not engender disgust. They also burn styrax to drive away the snakes which abound in the forests of perfume-producing trees.

XLI. These people have not got cinnamon or casia, and nevertheless Arabia is styled "Happy"—a country with a false and ungrateful appellation, as she puts her happiness to the credit of the powers above, although she owes more of it to the power below. Her good fortune has been caused by the luxury of mankind even in the hour of death, when they burn over the departed the products which they had originally understood to have been created for the gods. Good authorities declare that Arabia does not produce so large a quantity of perfume in a year's output as was burned by the Emperor Nero in a day at the obsequies of his consort Poppaea. Then reckon up the vast number of funerals celebrated yearly throughout the entire world, and the perfumes such as are given to the gods a grain at a time, that are piled up in heaps to the honour of dead bodies! Yet the gods used not to regard with less favour the worshippers who petitioned them with salted spelt, but rather, as the facts show, they were more benevolent in those days. But the title "happy" belongs still more to the Arabian Sea, for from it come the pearls which that country sends us. And by the lowest reckoning India, China and the Arabian peninsula take from our empire 100 million sesterces every year—that is the sum which our luxuries and our women cost us; for what fraction of these imports, I ask you, now goes to the gods or to the powers of the lower world?

Index

Aba, 58

Abha, 47, 97, 98, 100, 102

Ad, Lugman Bin, 74

Adz, 85-86, 87

Al Aunfudhah, 80

Al-Awami, Sheikh Shakeeb, 84

Al Beda: could qualify as important campsite, 49; only oasis, 64, 74; spring at, 65; camp in valley of Lemuel, 67; location of, 68, 77

Al Hijaz, 84

Al Humaydah, 63, 64

Al Kunfidah, 95, 102

Al-Rihab Hotel, 85

Ali, Shag'er, 98

Alma, 73

Amir of Iraq, 69

Amon, 53

Approach to the Book of Mormon, 24

Aqaba: shipyard town of, 50; population of, 60; eighteen miles between, and al Humaydah, 64; seventy-two miles from, to Al Beda, 77; shipping industry at, 114. *(See also* Gulf of Aqaba)

Arabia: history of, 16; shipping industry of, 87

Arabian coastal plain, 63

Arabian peninsula, 16, 40, 56; frankincense trade along, 29; frankincense indigenous to, 34; rule of asylum along, 57; goatskin bags used along, 58; now has no river of significance, 64; rainy season in, 65; rugs and blankets made on coast of, 99; not unpopulated wilderness, 115; travel along, 116

Arabian Sea, 40, 47

Archaeological Museum, Amman, Jordan, 95

Arnon, river and canyon, of, 65

Art forms of North and South American Indians, 116

Assyrians, 48

Awamir, 56

Azlan, 50

Babylon, 48

Bactrian camel, 91

Baghals, 87

Baghdad, 34

Bahrein, 43

Baskets, 99

Basterna, 102

Bay of Bengal, 114

Bedouin: tribes occupied Arabian peninsula, 28; life still resembles that of 2,600 years ago, 47; tents of, weigh 500 pounds, 52; camps, authors visit, 57-58; one-piece garment of, 58; describe survival skills, 59; youth talks about rainfall, 65; tents, construction of, 69; sheep taken to pasture, 74; life has not changed, 80; food, 83; fishing in Red Sea, 90; way of making bread, 90; practice of living off camels, 92; women express grief, 95; custom of praying, 97; women wear veils, 98; resemblance of, to Indians, 99-100

Beersheba, 56, 57, 69

Beit shaar, 68

Beka Valley in Lebanon, 56

Bellows, 110

Book of Deuteronomy, 48

Book of Mormon: quotations from, 17-21; fruits mentioned in, 71

Boom, 87

Bountiful, land of, 20, 40, 41, 51, 104-7; likely place for, 24; Nephi's description of, 27; eight years required to reach, 49; end of Lehi's trail from Jerusalem to, 115; is Salalah in Oman, 116

Bow, broken, 81-83

Breadmaking, 90

Building Nephi's ship, 20, 111-13

Burton, Sir Richard F., 84, 99

Caesar, Augustus, 100

Cairo, Egypt, 42, 49, 69, 90, 102

Cairo International Airport, 43

Camels, 53, 60, 67, 80, 91-92

Camp Tribulation, 82

Cannon, George Q., 52

Canton, China, 115

Canyon of the Arnon, 65

Ceylon, 114

Chaldeans, 48

Charcoal, 110

Children of Israel, 58, 105

China, 114

Chukri, Angie, 42, 102

Columbus, Christopher, 67

Crops, 70-71

San'a, 33
Sanau, 102
Sanbooq, 87
Sariah, 51, 52, 113
Saudi Arabian Ministry of
    Natural Resources, 33, 80
Sea of Galilee, 56
Sea of Weeds, 68
Seeb International Airport, 43
Semites, 58
Sennacherib, 58
Shanin, 59
Sharm-al-Sheikh, 64
Shazer, 19, 47, 50, 73; camp at,
    27; and place of broken bow,
    76
Sheba, 16, 101
Shipbuilding, 20, 28, 85-87,
    111-13, 116
Slings, 83
Smith, Joseph, 15, 21, 40, 51, 116
Snow, Erastus, 51
Solomon, 16, 32, 110, 111, 114
Somaliland, 41
South America, 115
South China Sea, 115
Southern Ocean, 40
Strabo, Greek historian, 28, 100,
    101
Straits of Hormuz, 114
Street vendors, 90
Styrax, 41
Suda, 95
Sultan of Oman, 44
Sur, 40
Syria, 38

Tahini, 90
Tents, 65-70
Thamud, 102
Theory, forming a, 21, 24
Thesiger, Wilfred, 40, 56, 91,
    102, 106
Thomas, Bertram, 24, 102, 106
Tihama, 63, 77, 85
Tiran, Straits of, 64
Tools, 107
Trail, meaning of word, 32
Trail, frankincense. *See*
    Frankincense trail
Trees, 106
Tribes of Dan and Asher, 114
Tubal Cain, 107

Umm Lajj, 100
United States Embassy, Muscat,
    44

Valley of Lemuel. *See* Lemuel,
    valley of
Van Beek, Gus W., 34
Vessel, ocean-going, 113-14
Visa, entry, to Saudi Arabia, 42

Wadi Ababish, 95
Wadi al 'Araba, 24, 49, 56, 60
Wadi al 'Arish, 65
Wadi Azlan, 50, 77
Wadi El Afal, 49, 63, 64, 65,
    67, 68, 74, 116
Wadi Umm Jurfayn, 63, 64, 65
Wadis, 38
Washington, D.C., 42
Water, 77-78
Waterbag, 59
Waterholes, 33
Weddings, 71-72
Wells, 98
Winds, favorable, 114-15
Wood, 106

Yam, 68
Yemen, 29, 34, 41, 64, 100, 101,
    112
Yenbo, 47, 59, 85, 86, 111, 112

Zaghreed, 95
Zedekiah, 48
Zipporah, 74
Zoram, 50, 51, 52, 71, 72